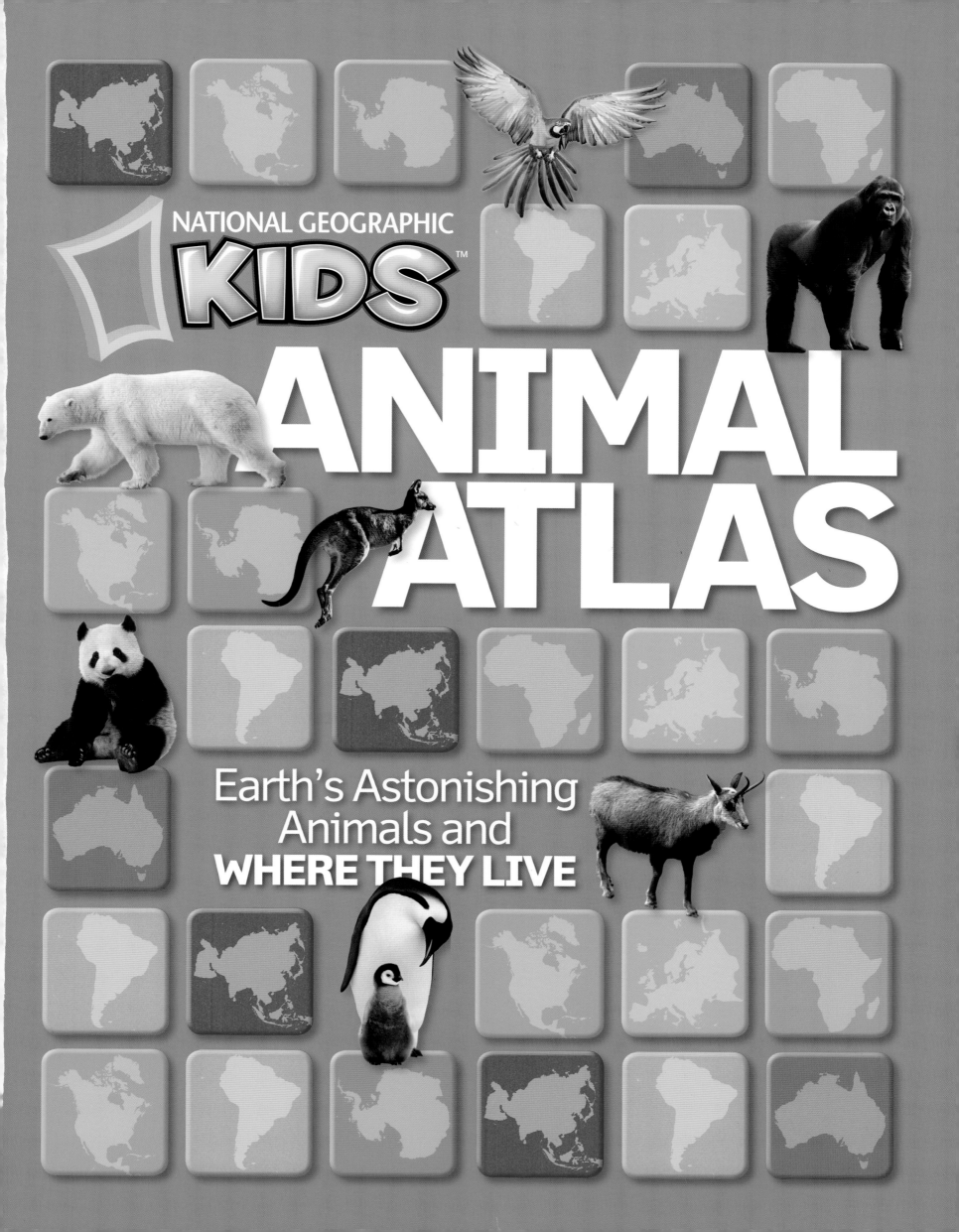

NATIONAL GEOGRAPHIC
KIDS™

ANIMAL ATLAS

Earth's Astonishing
Animals and
WHERE THEY LIVE

NATIONAL GEOGRAPHIC
KIDS

ANIMAL
ATLAS

Earth's Astonishing Animals and WHERE THEY LIVE

NATIONAL GEOGRAPHIC

WASHINGTON, D.C.

CONTENTS

ASIA
66

AFRICA
80

AUSTRALIA
94

ANTARCTICA
108

WHERE ANIMALS LIVE

We live in a world of animals, sharing the planet with millions of species. This book will help readers understand our animal friends and the world we all live on.

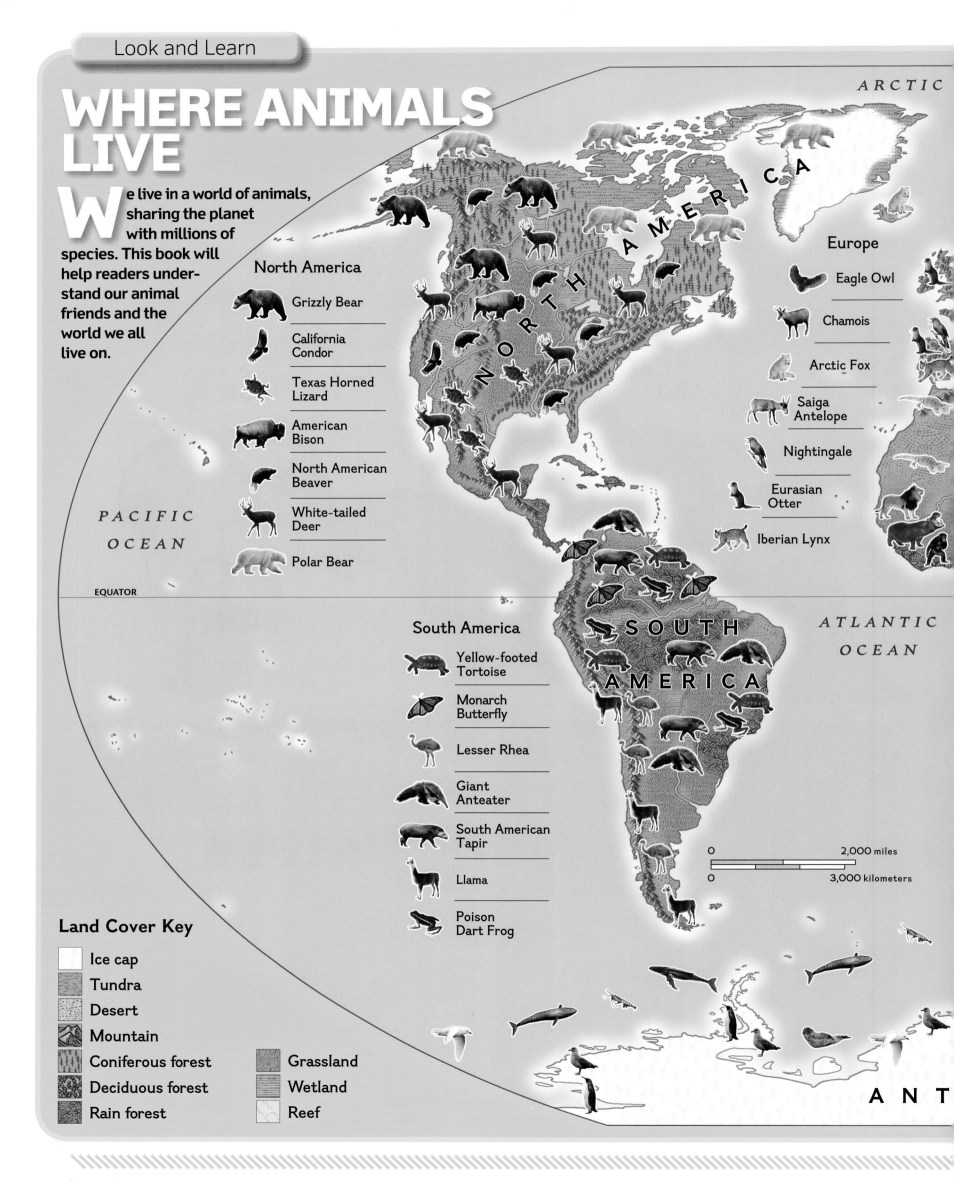

ARCTIC

NORTH AMERICA

Europe

Eagle Owl

Chamois

Arctic Fox

Saiga Antelope

Nightingale

Eurasian Otter

Iberian Lynx

North America

Grizzly Bear

California Condor

Texas Horned Lizard

American Bison

North American Beaver

White-tailed Deer

Polar Bear

PACIFIC OCEAN

EQUATOR

South America

Yellow-footed Tortoise

Monarch Butterfly

Lesser Rhea

Giant Anteater

South American Tapir

Llama

Poison Dart Frog

SOUTH AMERICA

ATLANTIC OCEAN

0   2,000 miles

0   3,000 kilometers

Land Cover Key

Ice cap

Tundra

Desert

Mountain

Coniferous forest   Grassland

Deciduous forest   Wetland

Rain forest   Reef

ANT

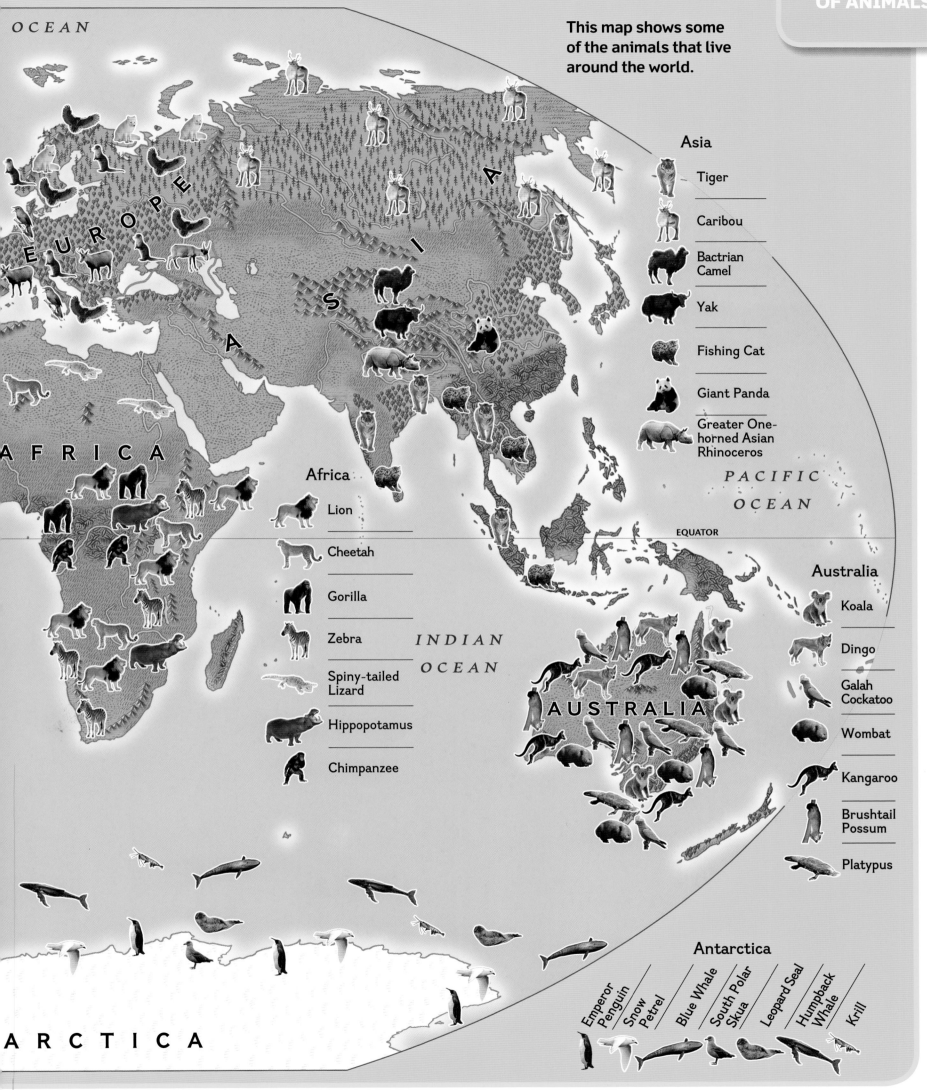

OCEAN

This map shows some of the animals that live around the world.

Asia
- Tiger
- Caribou
- Bactrian Camel
- Yak
- Fishing Cat
- Giant Panda
- Greater One-horned Asian Rhinoceros

PACIFIC OCEAN

EUROPE

A S I A

AFRICA

EQUATOR

Africa
- Lion
- Cheetah
- Gorilla
- Zebra
- Spiny-tailed Lizard
- Hippopotamus
- Chimpanzee

INDIAN OCEAN

AUSTRALIA

Australia
- Koala
- Dingo
- Galah Cockatoo
- Wombat
- Kangaroo
- Brushtail Possum
- Platypus

Antarctica
- Emperor Penguin
- Snow Petrel
- Blue Whale
- South Polar Skua
- Leopard Seal
- Humpback Whale
- Krill

ARCTICA

WHERE OCEAN ANIMALS LIVE

Earth is a water planet. More than 70 percent of its surface is covered by water, most of it salty. There are four great oceans—Arctic, Atlantic, Indian, and Pacific—with smaller extensions called bays, gulfs, and seas. And all of these water bodies are home to thousands of animals.

Ocean animals range in size from tiny **krill**—essential in the ocean food chain—to giants such as **gray whales.** Some ocean animals, such as the **clown fish,** sport brilliant colors while others living in the dark ocean depths are colorless.

Many ocean animals have developed fins that help them swim. Fish, such as the **Atlantic bluefin tuna,** have developed gills that allow them to breathe under water. Other animals, such as **elephant seals,** have lungs and must come to the surface for air.

Scientists have only begun to learn about Earth's oceans and the many creatures that live there. This map shows some of the marine life that lives in the world's oceans.

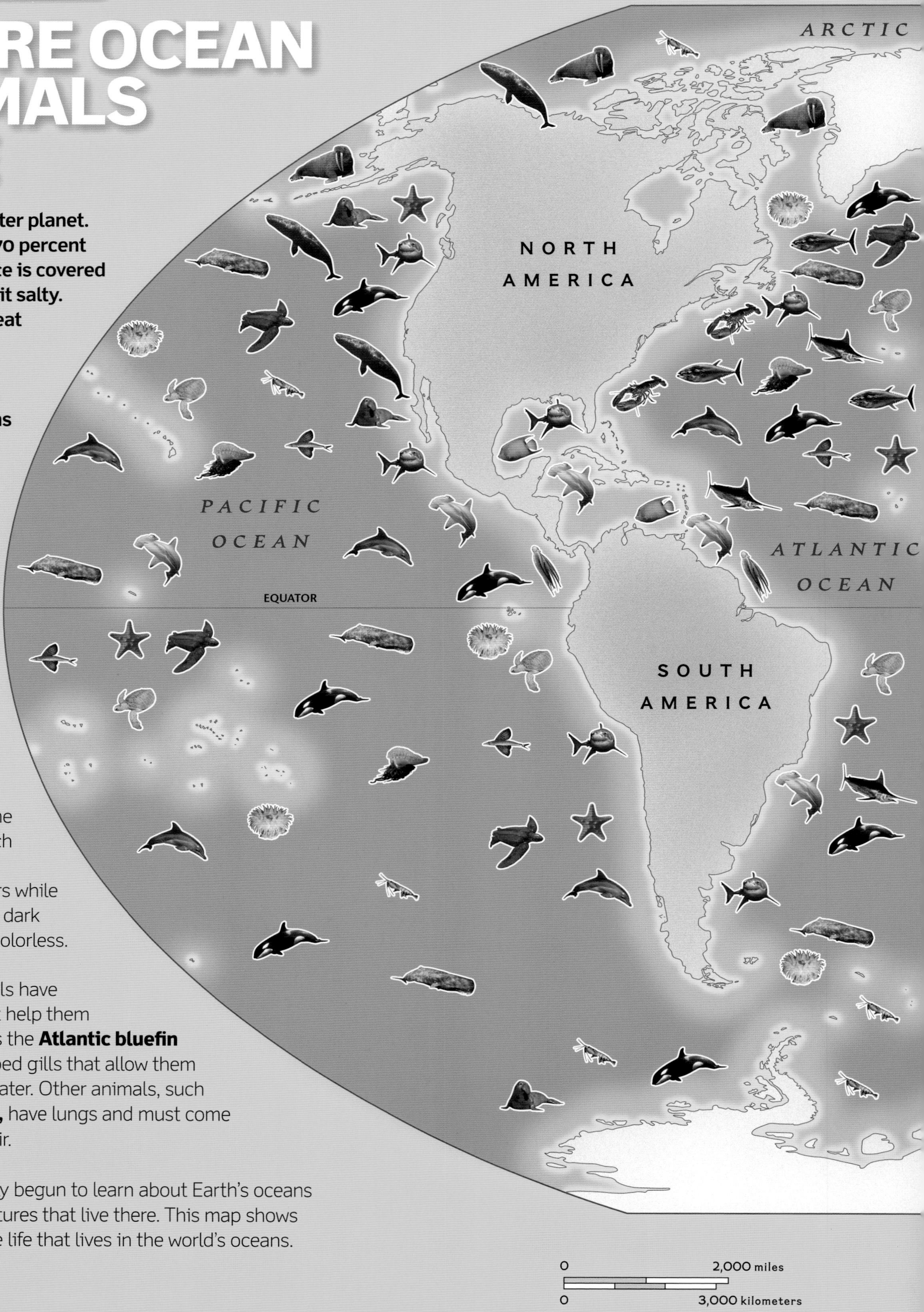

ARCTIC

NORTH AMERICA

PACIFIC OCEAN

ATLANTIC OCEAN

EQUATOR

SOUTH AMERICA

| 0 | | 2,000 miles |
| 0 | | 3,000 kilometers |

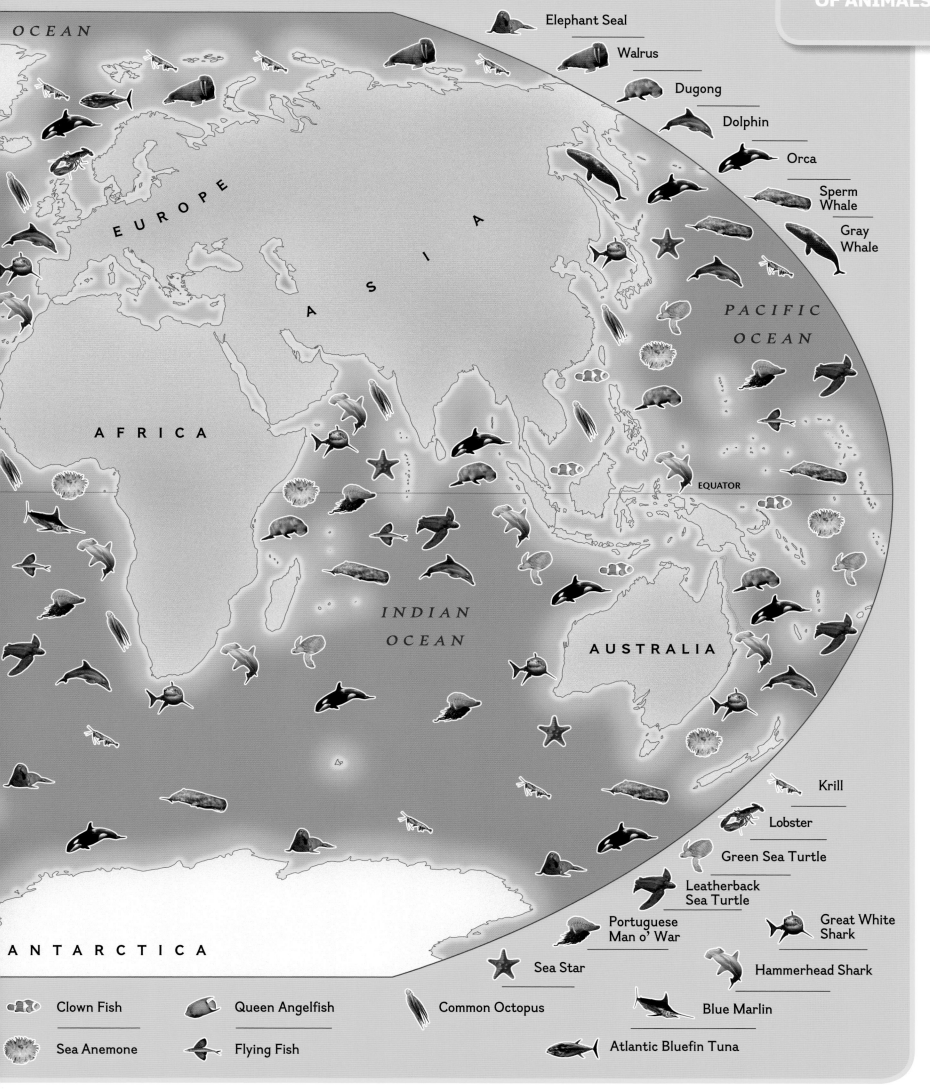

OCEAN

EUROPE

ASIA

AFRICA

PACIFIC OCEAN

EQUATOR

INDIAN OCEAN

AUSTRALIA

ANTARCTICA

Elephant Seal

Walrus

Dugong

Dolphin

Orca

Sperm Whale

Gray Whale

Krill

Lobster

Green Sea Turtle

Leatherback Sea Turtle

Portuguese Man o' War

Sea Star

Great White Shark

Hammerhead Shark

Blue Marlin

Clown Fish

Queen Angelfish

Common Octopus

Sea Anemone

Flying Fish

Atlantic Bluefin Tuna

ANIMAL ECOSYSTEMS

Earth is made up of many different ecosystems. An ecosystem is a special community of plants and animals that depend on each other. Below are examples of some of Earth's main ecosystems. Can you spot the animals listed below in the pictures?

ICE CAP This ecosystem, near Earth's Poles, is always cold. Only animals that have adapted, such as these **King Penguins** in Antarctica, can survive in this icy environment.

DESERT This dry ecosystem sometimes goes for years without rainfall. Animals such as this **Woma Python** near Ayers Rock in Australia survive with very little water.

TUNDRA Found on high mountains and near Earth's polar regions, this cold ecosystem has short summers. Animals such as the **Caribou** live in this harsh region.

MOUNTAIN The rocky landscape of this ecosystem is very challenging. Special hooves help animals such as these **Ibex** in the Italian Alps move quickly over the steep slopes.

FOREST Trees make up this ecosystem. Forests near the Equator, called rain forests, have many colorful birds, such as this **Scarlet Macaw** in the Amazon River Basin.

GRASSLAND Grasses, tall and short, make up this ecosystem. **Elephants,** such as these in Kenya's Masai Mara Reserve, are found in regions of tall tropical grasses called savanna.

WETLAND This ecosystem, which includes swamps and marshes, is covered with water at least part of each year. It is home to many animals, including this family of **Roe Deer**.

CORAL REEF This ecosystem is made up of millions of skeletons of tiny sea creatures, such as these **Stony Corals.** Colorful fish swim through Australia's Great Barrier Reef.

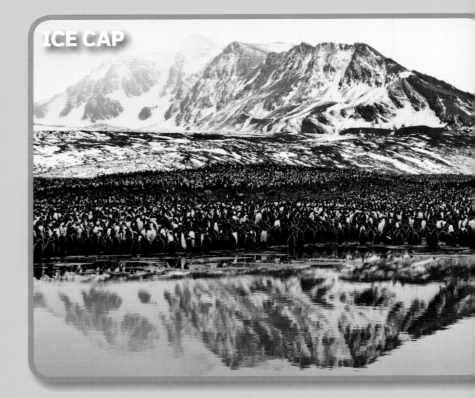

ICE CAP

MOUNTAIN

GRASSLAND

DESERT

TUNDRA

FOREST

WETLAND

CORAL REEF

ANIMAL HOMES

Animals, like people, live in many different types of homes. They live in trees, under rocks or logs, or even in holes in the ground. Find each animal below in its home at right.

WEB **Spiders** produce a silk-like substance from which they create webs that help them catch insects or even small birds.

CAVE A **Bengal Tiger** emerges from a dark cave in a rocky hillside in India. Caves provide natural shelter for this endangered animal.

DEN A young **Red Fox** stands in the entrance to its underground nest, called a den. Foxes use the same den for years.

SHELL Some animals, such as this **Snail,** carry their homes with them. When it senses danger, the snail just withdraws into its shell.

HIVE These **Western Honeybees** have built their home, which is called a hive, in the hollow trunk of a honey locust tree.

NEST This colorful **Masked Weaver Bird,** common throughout southern Africa, hangs upside down from its nest high in the treetop.

BURROW **Meerkats** live in complex underground burrows made up of tunnels and sleeping areas. A burrow may have as many as 70 entrances.

LODGE **Beavers** are nature's construction engineers. They build their homes, called lodges, using poles, sticks, and mud in ponds created by their dams.

ANEMONE The **Pink Anemonefish** lives safely among the stinging tentacles of the sea anemone, which lives in the reefs of the Pacific Ocean.

CAVE

ANEMONE

BURROW

WEB

DEN

HIVE

NEST

LODGE

SHELL

ANIMAL ADAPTATIONS

Many animals have developed special features that allow them to live successfully in different environments. These adaptations help animals survive in difficult terrain. Can you match the animal to its picture?

BEAKS The **Buff-tailed Coronet Humming-bird** uses its long, slender beak to reach into flowers for nectar, an important part of its diet.

HOOVES **Mountain Goats** have split hooves with rough pads that provide balance and grip, allowing them to move quickly over rugged mountainous terrain.

HEIGHT The **Giraffe's** long neck and legs—each 6 feet (1.8 meters)—enable it to eat leaves that are in the tops of trees.

CAMOUFLAGE The **Horned Leaf Chameleon** can change its color as a form of defense to hide from predators. Here it is almost invisible on a brown leaf.

BODY ARMOR When threatened, the **Porcupinefish** inflates its body with either water or air, extending sharp spines that can be poisonous.

COLOR Some animals, such as the vivid **Milkweed Grasshopper,** wear bright colors to warn predators that they are poisonous.

WINGS The **Bald Eagle** uses its talons to catch fish and its broad, powerful wings to soar up from the water's surface.

HIBERNATION In winter **Greater Horseshoe Bats** hang upside down from the ceilings of caves or old buildings in an extended sleep called hibernation.

WEBBED FEET **Ducks** spend much of their lives in water. Their webbed feet act like flippers, helping them paddle smoothly through the water.

BEAKS

CAMOUFLAGE

WINGS

HOOVES

HEIGHT

BODY ARMOR

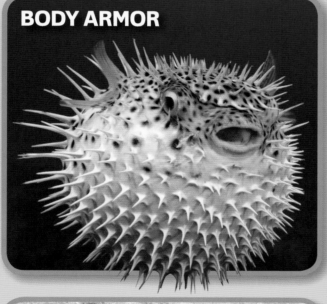

COLOR

HIBERNATION

WEBBED FEET

ANIMAL MIGRATIONS

Most of Earth's animals live within a relatively small area, traveling only a few miles from their nest or den to find food and water. But some animals travel thousands of miles in a movement called migration.

Some animals migrate from very cold places to places with milder weather. **Caribou** spend summer months in the tundra, but as winter approaches, they move south to the forests of the taiga where there is better food and shelter. The **Arctic Tern** travels thousands of miles from Pole to Pole, following northern and southern summer seasons.

In Africa's eastern grasslands, vast herds of **Wildebeest**—up to one million animals—move north and south following seasonal rains and fresh grazing lands. In the Atlantic and Pacific Oceans, **Humpback Whales** spend summers in cold, nutrient-rich waters near the Arctic Ocean but migrate south to warmer waters in winter.

Leatherback Sea Turtles migrate from deep ocean waters to coastal beaches where they lay their eggs before returning to the sea.

Check out this map to see sample migration routes of these travelers and other animals on the move.

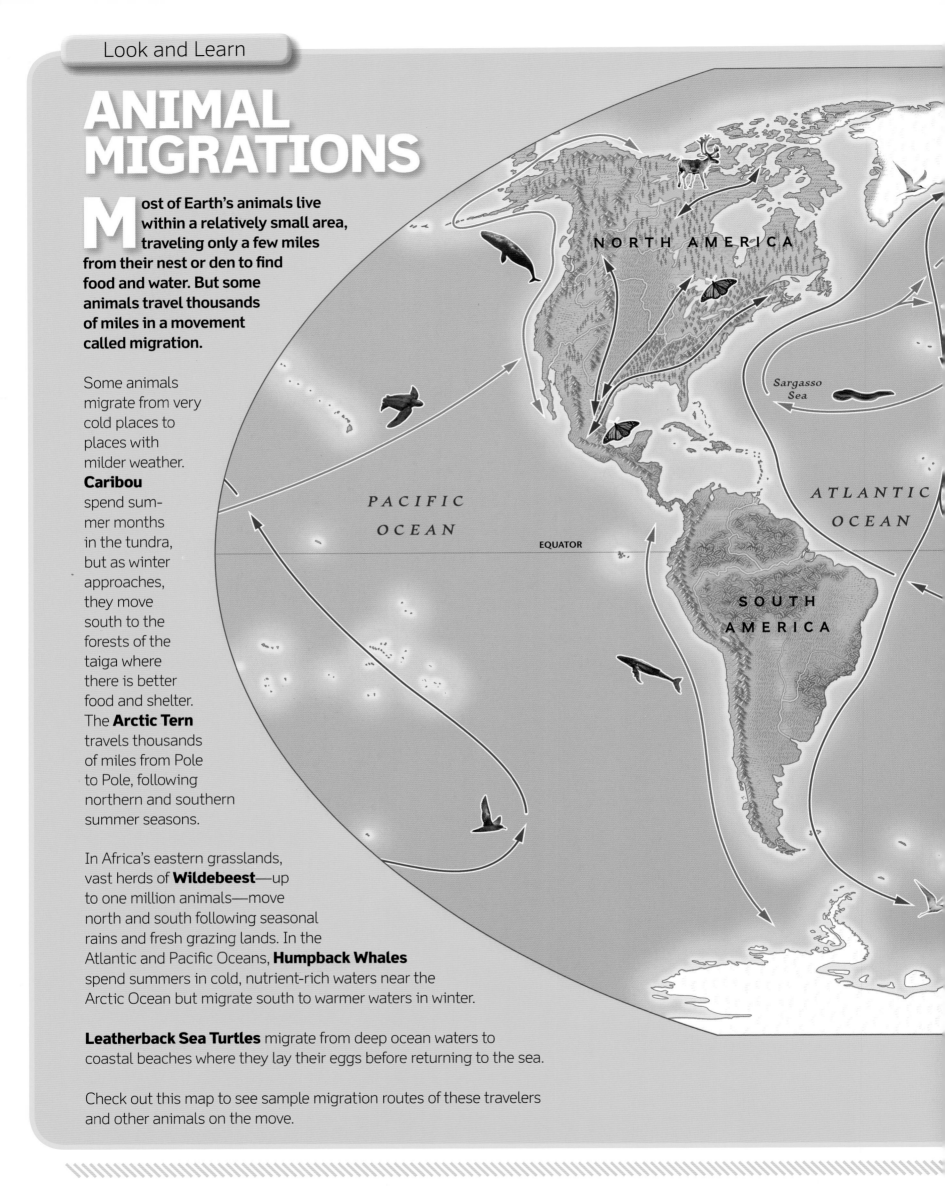

NORTH AMERICA

Sargasso Sea

PACIFIC OCEAN

EQUATOR

ATLANTIC OCEAN

SOUTH AMERICA

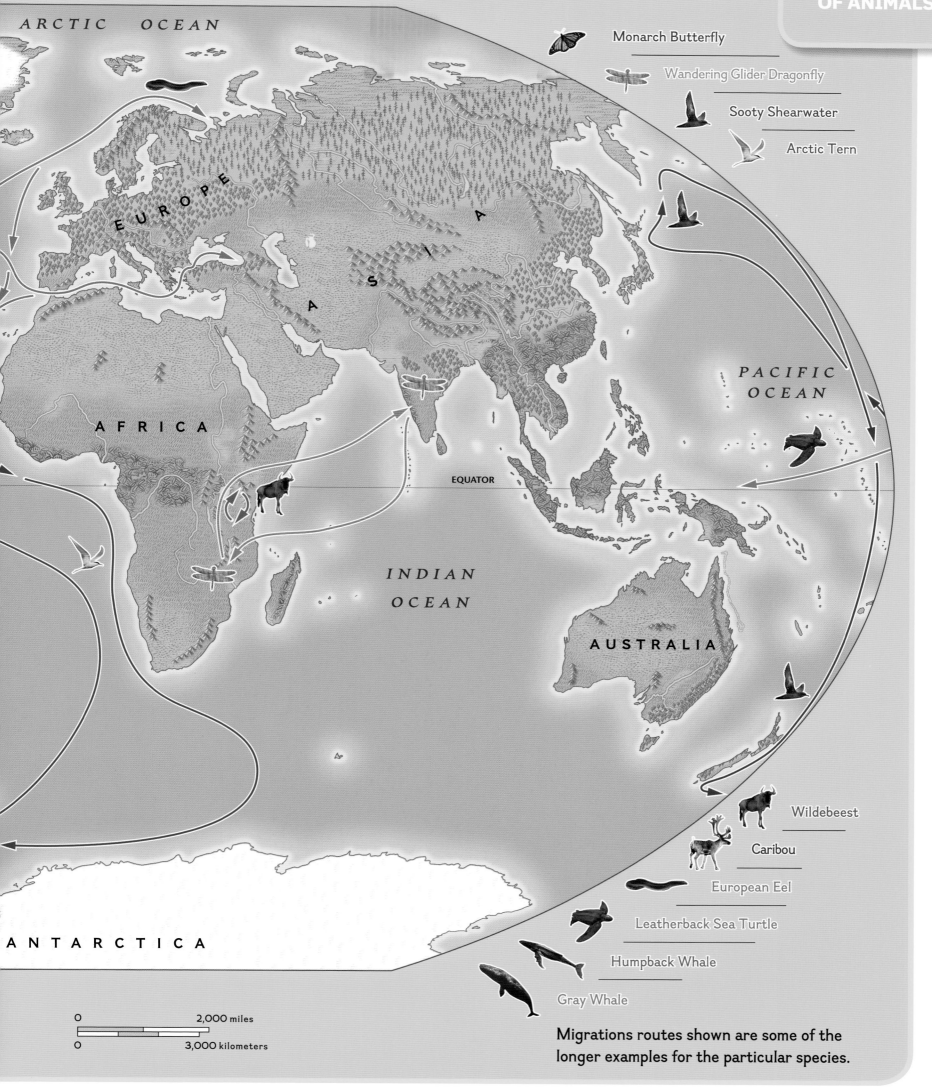

ARCTIC OCEAN

Monarch Butterfly

Wandering Glider Dragonfly

Sooty Shearwater

Arctic Tern

EUROPE

ASIA

PACIFIC
OCEAN

AFRICA

EQUATOR

INDIAN
OCEAN

AUSTRALIA

Wildebeest

Caribou

European Eel

Leatherback Sea Turtle

Humpback Whale

ANTARCTICA

Gray Whale

0   2,000 miles

0   3,000 kilometers

Migrations routes shown are some of the
longer examples for the particular species.

ENDANGERED ANIMALS

H umans and animals share most natural environments, but the activities of humans have put some animals at risk. We alter ecosystems by creating air, water, and soil pollution; by farming; building cities; and mining; and by hunting for food or sport. This puts some animals in danger. Here are some animals we need to watch and protect.

WHOOPING CRANE In 1941 there were only 16 whooping cranes living. Due to conservation efforts, the population is now over 400, but this bird remains at risk because the land it lives on is being destroyed.

TASMANIAN DEVIL This mammal is found only on Tasmania, Australia's island state. Killed off in mainland Australia in the 1800s by farmers, they are now at risk due to a rare disease.

SUMATRAN ORANGUTAN The clearing of tropical forests for logging and farming has taken away the natural habitat of this tree-dwelling great ape, resulting in an 80 percent reduction of the original population.

FOSSA This cat-like relative of the mongoose lives in the forests of Madagascar. Only about ten percent of this island's forests remain, so the fossa is endangered because its habitat is shrinking.

GALAPAGOS PENGUIN These warm weather penguins eat fish and crustaceans found in the cold waters of the Humboldt Current. A diminished food supply in recent years has put these birds at risk.

MEDITERRANEAN MONK SEAL Only about 600 of these shy seals remain. They are killed by fishermen for their oil and meat. They are also threatened by industrial pollution and development along coasts.

BLUE WHALE These giants of the oceans nearly became extinct in the 1900s when they were killed for valuable whale oil. Now they are protected, but many are still injured in accidents with ships.

WHOOPING CRANE

FOSSA

MEDITERRANEAN MONK SEAL

TASMANIAN DEVIL

SUMATRAN
ORANGUTAN

GALAPAGOS PENGUIN

BLUE WHALE

ANIMAL PRESERVES

Many animals are at risk because of loss of habitat, pollution, diminished food supply, or climate change. One way people are protecting these animals is through creation of preserves and parks where human activity is controlled and animals can live in their natural environment. These protected areas account for about 11 percent of Earth's land area.

Florida's **Everglades National Park** offers a safe environment for wetland animals, including the **Florida Panther.** The **Barrier Reef Reserve System** in Belize protects many sea creatures, including the **Long Snout Seahorse.**

The **Península Valdés Reserve** in Argentina provides safe habitat for marine mammals, including the **Southern Elephant Seal.**

The **Camargue Biosphere Reserve**, in France's Rhône River delta, offers safe habitat for wetland animals, including the **Camargue Horse.**

In **Malaysia's Danum Valley Conservation Area,** rain forest animals, including the **Clouded Leopard,** are protected.

Kenya's **Masai Mara National Park** allows tourists to see many of Africa's wild animals, including the wide-eyed **Bushbaby.**

Kakadu National Park in northern Australia provides safe habitat for the colorful **Gouldian Finch.**

Although it has no permanent population, **Antarctica** is like a vast frozen preserve because its wildlife is protected by the Antarctic Treaty.

FLORIDA PANTHER

LONG SNOUT SEAHORSE

SOUTHERN ELEPHANT SEAL

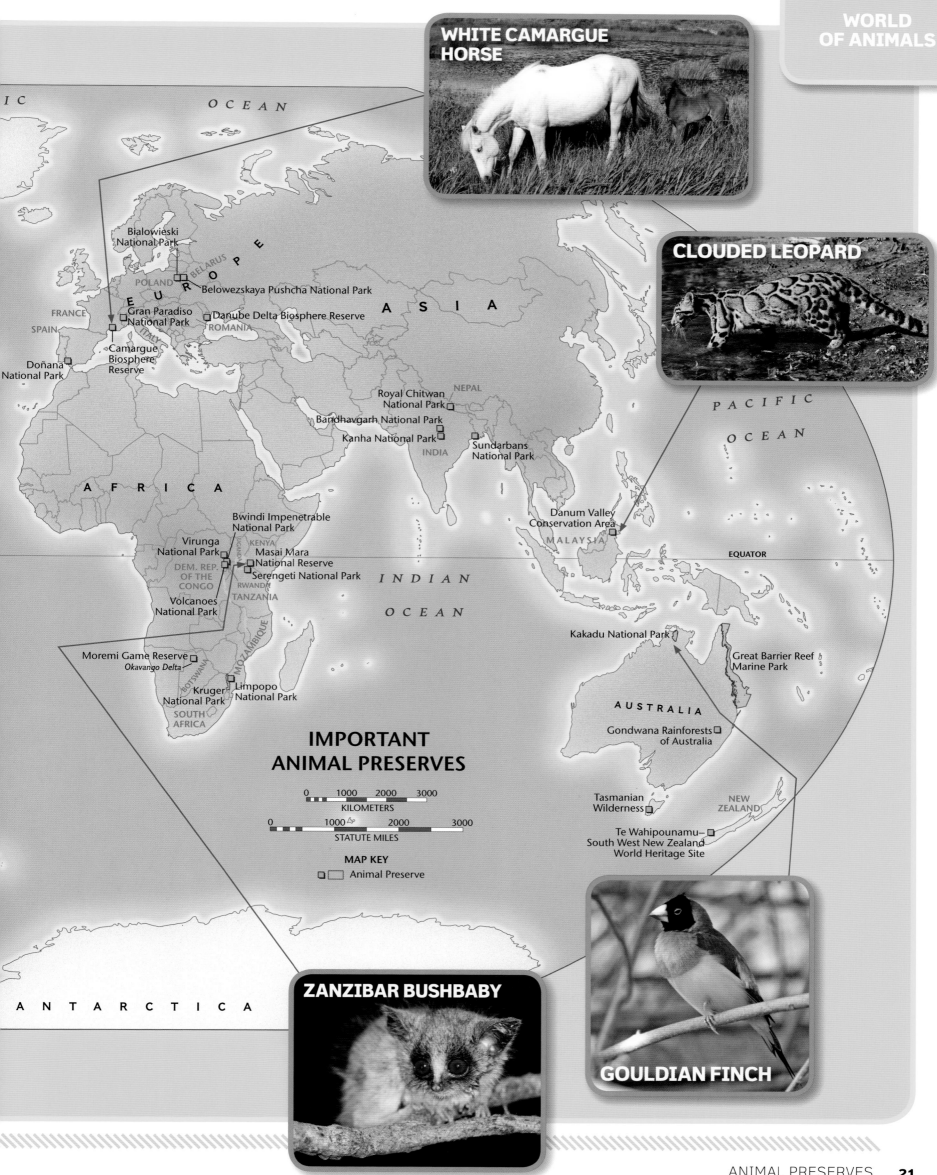

**WHITE CAMARGUE
HORSE**

CLOUDED LEOPARD

OCEAN

OCEAN

Bialowieski
National Park

BELARUS

POLAND

Belowezskaya Pushcha National Park

E U R O P E

A S I A

Gran Paradiso
National Park

FRANCE

Danube Delta Biosphere Reserve

SPAIN

ROMANIA

Camargue
Biosphere
Reserve

Doñana
National Park

NEPAL

PACIFIC

OCEAN

Royal Chitwan
National Park

Bandhavgarh National Park

Kanha National Park

A F R I C A

INDIA

Sundarbans
National Park

Bwindi Impenetrable
National Park

Danum Valley
Conservation Area

Virunga
National Park

KENYA

MALAYSIA

DEM. REP.
OF THE
CONGO

Masai Mara
National Reserve

EQUATOR

Serengeti National Park

RWANDA

Volcanoes
National Park

TANZANIA

I N D I A N

O C E A N

Kakadu National Park

Moremi Game Reserve
Okavango Delta

MOZAMBIQUE

Great Barrier Reef
Marine Park

BOTSWANA

Kruger
National Park

Limpopo
National Park

A U S T R A L I A

SOUTH
AFRICA

Gondwana Rainforests
of Australia

IMPORTANT
ANIMAL PRESERVES

Tasmanian
Wilderness

NEW
ZEALAND

| 0 | 1000 | 2000 | 3000 |
KILOMETERS

| 0 | 1000 | 2000 | 3000 |
STATUTE MILES

Te Wahipounamu–
South West New Zealand
World Heritage Site

MAP KEY

☐ ☐ Animal Preserve

A N T A R C T I C A

ZANZIBAR BUSHBABY

GOULDIAN FINCH

ANIMALS AND PEOPLE

From earliest times, people have had a special relationship with animals. Dogs are our companions. Lions are symbols of national power. And animals often appear on flags, currency, or emblems.

The **Bald Eagle**, which appears on the Great Seal, has been the national emblem of the United States since 1782.

The **Andean Condor** has appeared in Andean art for more than 4,000 years. It can be seen on coins in Chile and Colombia.

The **Brown Bear,** found across northern Europe, was the mascot— *Misha*—during the 1980 Summer Olympic Games in the USSR, now Russia.

The **Markhor,** a wild sheep with heavy spiral horns, is the national animal of Pakistan. It also appears on a 1989 stamp printed in Afghanistan.

The colorful coat of arms for Madagascar includes the head of a **Zebu,** a type of cattle found in many tropical countries.

On the back of Australia's fifty cent coin is the national coat of arms, which includes a **Kangaroo** and an **Emu,** both animals unique to this continent.

You can use this political map to match animal ranges shown throughout the book to countries around the world. What animals live near you?

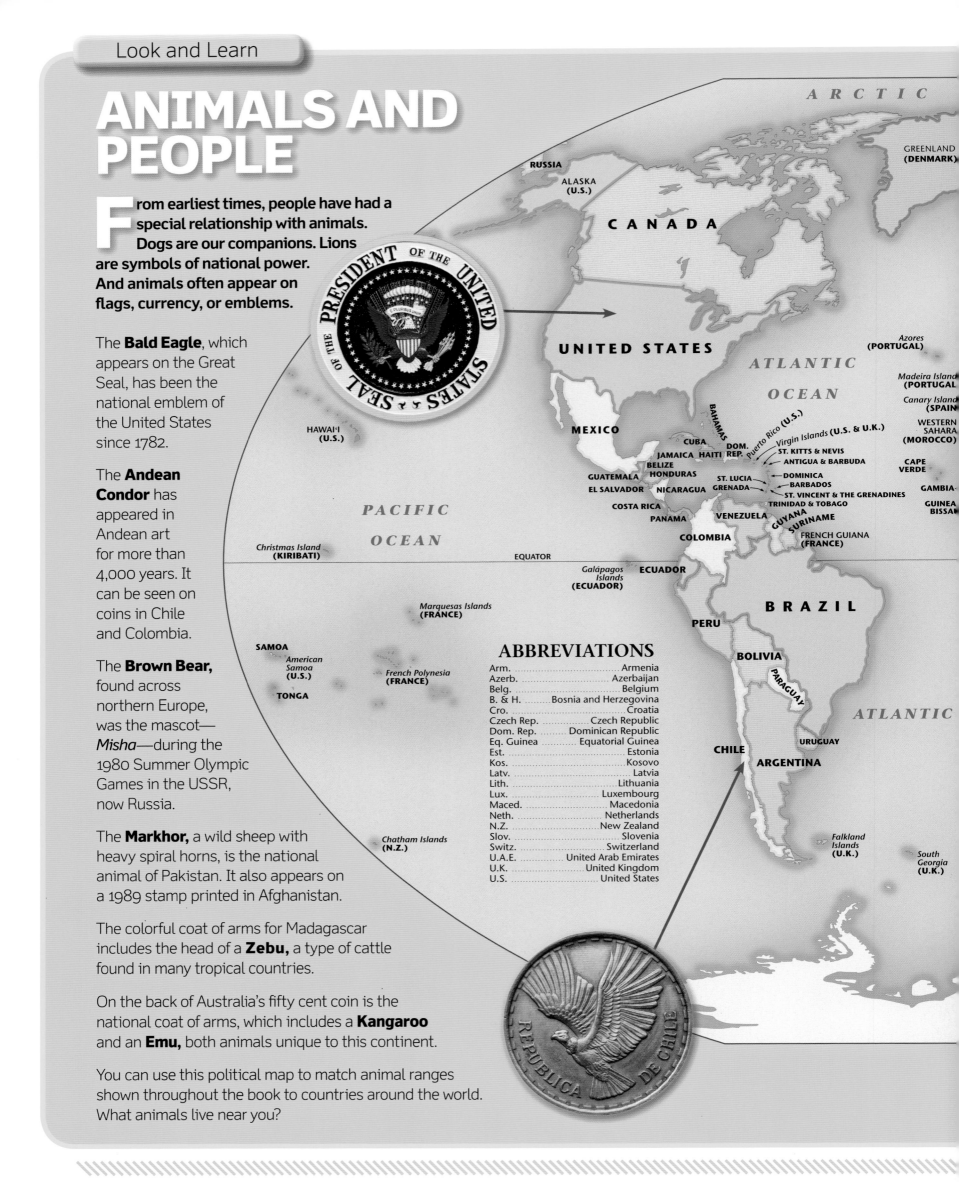

ABBREVIATIONS

Arm.	Armenia
Azerb.	Azerbaijan
Belg.	Belgium
B. & H.	Bosnia and Herzegovina
Cro.	Croatia
Czech Rep.	Czech Republic
Dom. Rep.	Dominican Republic
Eq. Guinea	Equatorial Guinea
Est.	Estonia
Kos.	Kosovo
Latv.	Latvia
Lith.	Lithuania
Lux.	Luxembourg
Maced.	Macedonia
Neth.	Netherlands
N.Z.	New Zealand
Slov.	Slovenia
Switz.	Switzerland
U.A.E.	United Arab Emirates
U.K.	United Kingdom
U.S.	United States

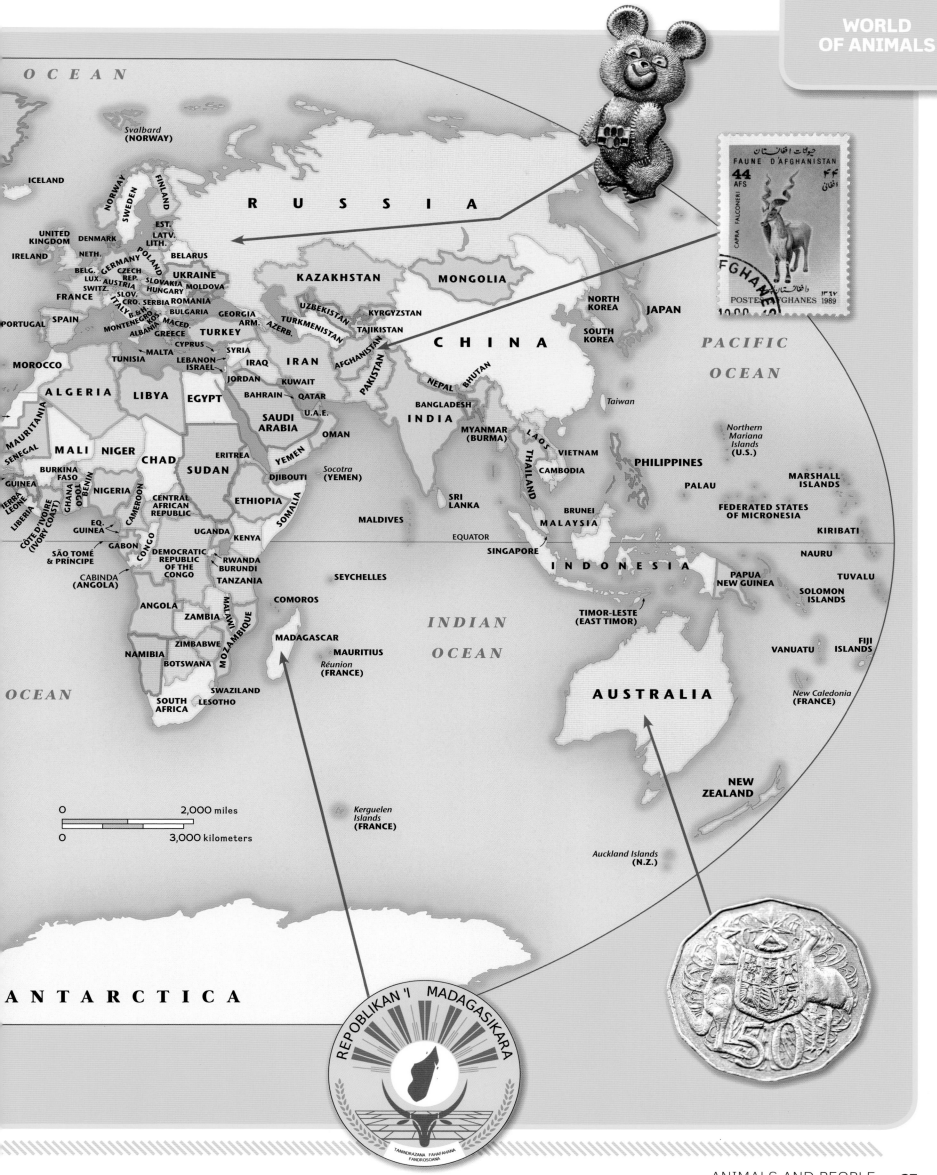

OCEAN

ICELAND

Svalbard
(NORWAY)

NORWAY

SWEDEN

FINLAND

UNITED
KINGDOM

IRELAND

DENMARK

EST.
LATV.
LITH.

BELARUS

NETH.

GERMANY

POLAND

BELG.
LUX. AUSTRIA
SWITZ.
FRANCE

CZECH
REP.
SLOVAKIA
MOLDOVA
HUNGARY
SLOV.
CRO. SERBIA ROMANIA
B. & H.

UKRAINE

RUSSIA

KAZAKHSTAN

MONGOLIA

NORTH
KOREA

JAPAN

PORTUGAL

SPAIN

ITALY
MONTENEGRO
ALBANIA
GREECE

KOS.
MACED.
BULGARIA

GEORGIA
ARM.
AZERB.

TURKEY

CYPRUS

UZBEKISTAN

TURKMENISTAN

KYRGYZSTAN

TAJIKISTAN

CHINA

SOUTH
KOREA

PACIFIC

OCEAN

MOROCCO

TUNISIA

MALTA

LEBANON
ISRAEL

SYRIA

IRAQ

IRAN

AFGHANISTAN

JORDAN

KUWAIT

PAKISTAN

NEPAL

BHUTAN

Taiwan

ALGERIA

LIBYA

EGYPT

BAHRAIN

QATAR

SAUDI
ARABIA

U.A.E.

OMAN

BANGLADESH

INDIA

MYANMAR
(BURMA)

LAOS

VIETNAM

Northern
Mariana
Islands
(U.S.)

MAURITANIA

MALI

NIGER

CHAD

SUDAN

ERITREA

YEMEN

Socotra
(YEMEN)

THAILAND

CAMBODIA

PHILIPPINES

PALAU

MARSHALL
ISLANDS

SENEGAL

BURKINA
FASO

NIGERIA

DJIBOUTI

SRI
LANKA

BRUNEI

FEDERATED STATES
OF MICRONESIA

GUINEA

BENIN

CAMEROON

CENTRAL
AFRICAN
REPUBLIC

ETHIOPIA

SOMALIA

MALDIVES

MALAYSIA

KIRIBATI

SIERRA
LEONE

GHANA
TOGO

CÔTE D'IVOIRE
(IVORY COAST)

EQ.
GUINEA

UGANDA

KENYA

EQUATOR

NAURU

LIBERIA

GABON

CONGO

SÃO TOMÉ
& PRÍNCIPE

DEMOCRATIC
REPUBLIC
OF THE
CONGO

RWANDA
BURUNDI

SINGAPORE

INDONESIA

PAPUA
NEW GUINEA

TUVALU

CABINDA
(ANGOLA)

TANZANIA

SEYCHELLES

SOLOMON
ISLANDS

ANGOLA

ZAMBIA

MALAWI

MOZAMBIQUE

COMOROS

MADAGASCAR

MAURITIUS

INDIAN

OCEAN

TIMOR-LESTE
(EAST TIMOR)

VANUATU

FIJI
ISLANDS

NAMIBIA

ZIMBABWE

BOTSWANA

Réunion
(FRANCE)

New Caledonia
(FRANCE)

OCEAN

SOUTH
AFRICA

SWAZILAND

LESOTHO

AUSTRALIA

0   2,000 miles

0   3,000 kilometers

Kerguelen
Islands
(FRANCE)

NEW
ZEALAND

Auckland Islands
(N.Z.)

ANTARCTICA

FAUNE D'AFGHANISTAN
44
AFS
CAPRA FALCONERI
POSTES AFGHANES 1989

REPOBLIKAN 'I   MADAGASIKARA
TANINDRAZANA FAHAFAHANA
FANDROSOANA

DESPITE THEIR
IMPRESSIVE SIZE,
GRIZZLIES
ARE QUITE **FAST**
AND HAVE
BEEN CLOCKED AT
30 MILES
(48 KILOMETERS)
AN HOUR.

NORTH AMERICA

North America is **9,449,000 square miles (24,474,000 square kilometers)** in area. It is the third largest continent and makes up almost 17 percent of Earth's land area. It stretches from ice caps and tundras in the north to tropical forests in the south, with grasslands, wetlands, mountains, and deserts in between. These ecosystems are home to many animals, including this Grizzly Bear trying to catch a salmon in a river in Alaska.

NORTH AMERICA

California Condor

Texas Horned Lizard

American Bison

ASIA

PACIFIC OCEAN

North American Beaver

White-tailed Deer

Polar Bear

North America is made up of many different ecosystems. Thousands of different animals live on the land, in the skies, or in the waters of the continent, and they have special features that help them survive in their environments.

ICE CAP AND TUNDRA This frozen region is home to many Arctic animals, including the Polar Bear. This giant mammal hunts seals in the icy waters of the north. Rising ocean temperatures and melting ice may put polar bears at risk by disrupting their food supply.

DESERT The Texas Horned Lizard is a fierce-looking member of the reptile family with numerous "horns" on its head and back. It eats mainly insects and lives in burrows in dry regions with very little vegetation.

MOUNTAIN California Condors live in rocky cliffs in the western mountains of North America. These huge birds can fly as high as 15,000 feet (4,572 meters). Condors are nature's housekeepers because they eat dead animals. Condors are an endangered species.

FOREST White-tailed Deer live mainly in forests and meadows of North America. The male deer, called a buck, can be identified by its antlers. White-tailed deer graze mainly at dawn or dusk and eat leaves, grasses, and twigs.

GRASSLAND Much of central North America is grassland, where animals such as the American Bison graze in herds. Bison were hunted almost to extinction in the 1800s.

WETLAND The North American Beaver, North America's largest rodent, is found throughout the region. Beavers are skilled engineers. They build dams out of mud, stones, and sticks in rivers and ponds.

Land Cover Key

- Ice cap
- Tundra
- Desert
- Mountain
- Coniferous forest
- Deciduous forest
- Rain forest
- Grassland
- Wetland

ARCTIC OCEAN

Greenland

Iceland (EUROPE)

Alaska

ATLANTIC OCEAN

Hudson Bay

ROCKY MOUNTAINS

CANADIAN SHIELD

GREAT PLAINS

Appalachian Mountntains

Sierra Nevada

Red dot indicates an animal at risk.*

Grizzly Bear

California Condor ●

Texas Horned Lizard

American Bison

North American Beaver

White-tailed Deer

Polar Bear ●

Gulf of Mexico

W E S T   I N D I E S

Caribbean Sea

Central America

0   500 miles
0   750 kilometers

*Animals that are at risk are in danger of no longer being found in the wild because of loss of habitat or danger from humans.

SOUTH AMERICA

THE SONORAN DESERT

The Sonoran Desert covers 120,000 square miles (310,799 square kilometers) in the southwestern United States and northwestern Mexico. It is the hottest North American desert, but seasonal rains support a wide variety of plant and animal life. Here are some of the animals that live in the Sonoran Desert.

UNITED STATES

PACIFIC OCEAN

MEXICO

Sonoran Desert

0   200 miles

0   200 kilometers

2.52

0.52 *0.51 0.67 0.23 0.12 0.33 1.61 1.12 1.10 0.85 0.89
JAN FEB MAR APR MAY JUN JUL AUG SEP OCT NOV DEC
* Average inches of rainfall per month

RAINFALL IN THE SONORAN DESERT

GILA WOODPECKER
This bird often nests in a hole made with its sharp beak in a Saguaro cactus.

WESTERN DIAMONDBACK RATTLESNAKE
The Western Diamondback is the largest rattler living in the Sonoran Desert. Its venom can be deadly.

BANDED GILA MONSTER
This desert reptile is one of just two poisonous lizards found in North America.

Animal at risk

TURKEY VULTURE
These birds, with a wingspan of 6 feet (almost 2 meters), feed mainly on dead animals.

ANIMAL BITES

WHEN FLOWERS ARE IN BLOOM IN THE SONORAN DESERT, **BEES & BIRDS** POLLINATE THEM DURING THE DAY. AT NIGHT, **BATS** TAKE OVER THE JOB.

DESERT BIGHORN SHEEP
Desert bighorns have padded hooves that enable them to move quickly over steep, rocky terrain.

SONORAN PRONGHORN
Sharp eyesight and great speed protect this endangered animal from desert predators such as wolves.

BOBCAT
These felines live throughout North America, including desert areas. Because they hunt at night, bobcats are rarely seen.

GREATER ROADRUNNER
This desert bird rarely flies, but can run as fast as 15 miles (24 kilometers) an hour.

THE EVERGLADES

The Everglades is a vast wetland area that covers more than 5,000 square miles (112,950 square kilometers) of south Florida. Water flows through this "River of Grass"—home to many animals—from Lake Okeechobee all the way to Florida Bay. Here are some of the animals that live in the Everglades.

ANIMAL BITES

MORE THAN **300 SPECIES** OF **BIRDS** AND MORE THAN **1,000 SPECIES** OF **PLANTS** LIVE IN EVERGLADES NATIONAL PARK.

ALABAMA GEORGIA

FLORIDA

ATLANTIC OCEAN

GULF OF MEXICO

Lake Okeechobee

■ The Everglades

0   100 miles
0   100 kilometers

Florida Bay
Florida Keys

THE EVERGLADES WATER CYCLE

Precipitation

Lake Okeechobee

Runoff

River

Swamp

Freshwater Marsh

Wetlands

Wetlands

Saltwater Marsh

Estuary

Spring

Evaporation

Groundwater

Gulf of Mexico

AMERICAN BLACK BEAR
These bears mainly eat grasses, fruits, and nuts, but they also raid garbage cans for human food.

EVERGLADES MINK
This member of the weasel family is a meat-eating animal that stalks its prey at night.

GREEN SEA TURTLE
These turtles are the largest of all hard shelled turtles. They feed primarily on sea grasses and algae.

Animal at risk

GREAT BLUE HERON
Largest of all North American herons, these birds mainly eat fish but also catch lizards, frogs, and snakes.

ROSEATE SPOONBILL
This large wading bird swings its wide bill back and forth in the water to catch small fish.

WATER MOCCASIN
This snake has poisonous venom, but seldom bites unless stepped on. It is also known as a cottonmouth.

AMERICAN ALLIGATOR
Scientists believe this dangerous and fierce-looking creature has lived on Earth for more than 150 million years.

NORTH AMERICAN GRAY FOX
The very agile gray fox is the only member of the dog family that can climb a tree.

POLAR BEARS

Polar bears are large, fierce land predators. Males, rising on hind legs, can stand up to ten feet (three meters) tall. Despite their size, they can run up to 25 miles (40 kilometers) per hour over short distances. Polar bears live in the bitterly cold environment above the Arctic Circle. Two layers of fur over a thick layer of fat called blubber protect polar bears from temperatures that fall well below freezing during the dark Arctic winters.

Polar bears hunt from ice floes in the frigid waters of the Arctic Ocean. Thick fur and a layer of fat protect them from the cold.

HABITAT Polar bears live along the edges of the Arctic Ocean and on sea ice that stretches out over the cold ocean waters. Most polar bears are found in the Arctic regions of Alaska, Canada, Greenland, Norway, and Russia.

DIET The main food source for polar bears is the ringed seal. Seals cut breathing holes in the ice in order to come up for air. Polar bears wait patiently by these holes until seals pop up. Then they catch the seals with a swipe of their large paws.

SURVIVAL Polar bears were once hunted as trophies. But a greater risk today is posed by climate change. Sea ice in the Arctic is melting, reducing the hunting area of polar bears and putting their food supply at risk.

FACTS AT A GLANCE

RANGE Coastal areas along the Arctic Ocean in Alaska and Canada, as well as Greenland, Norway, and Russia

LIFE SPAN 20 to 30 years in the wild

SIZE Males: 660 to 1,760 pounds (300 to 800 kilograms); Females: 330 to 660 pounds (150 to 300 kilograms)

DIET Primarily ringed seals

Polar bears usually have two cubs, which are hairless and blind at birth. Cubs remain with their mother until they are about two years old.

A young polar bear stands among colorful fireweed and stares intently across the landscape. The bear's sensitive nose can smell seal on the ice up to 20 miles (32 kilometers) away.

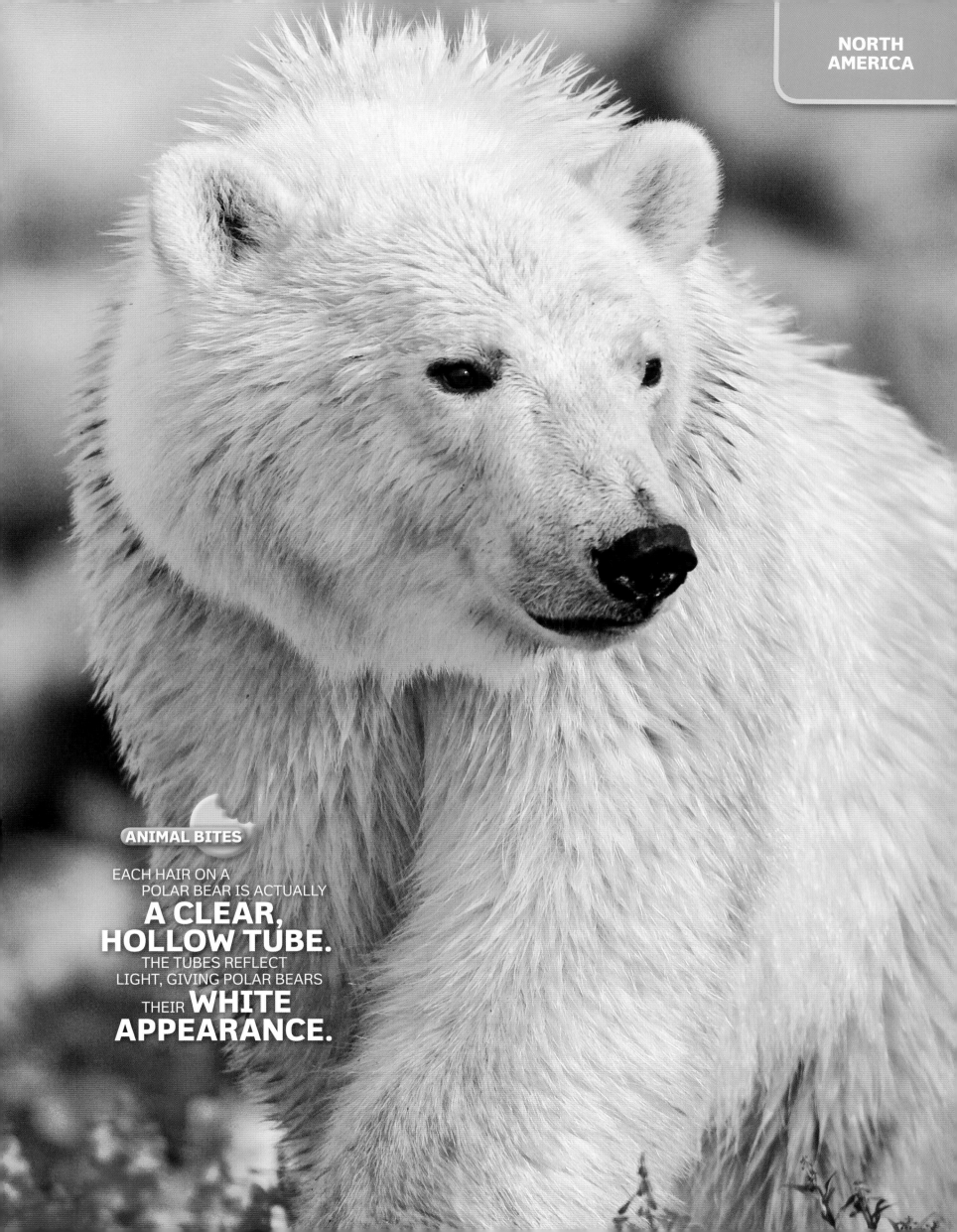

ANIMAL BITES

EACH HAIR ON A
POLAR BEAR IS ACTUALLY
**A CLEAR,
HOLLOW TUBE.**
THE TUBES REFLECT
LIGHT, GIVING POLAR BEARS
THEIR **WHITE
APPEARANCE.**

ANIMAL BITES

AMERICAN **BISON** USE THEIR **HEADS** TO **DIG** THROUGH **DEEP SNOW** TO REACH THE VEGETATION BELOW. THEY HAVE POOR EYESIGHT, BUT AN **EXCELLENT** SENSE OF **SMELL.**

Spotlight on

AMERICAN BISON

A bison calf stays close to its mother. Calves weigh 30 to 70 pounds (14 to 32 kilograms) at birth.

Snow clings to a bison's face in Yellowstone National Park. The animal's shaggy hair protects it from the bitter cold of winter.

The American bison is a symbol of North America's frontier history. As many as 60 million bison may have roamed the grasslands of the Great Plains when Europeans first arrived. Most of the bison we see today are a product of breeding managed by conservationists. Although sometimes mistakenly called a buffalo, the bison is actually a relative of cattle and goats. Bison are the heaviest land animals in North America. They are considered to be more dangerous than a grizzly bear because they sometimes attack for no apparent reason, using their horns, their large skull, and their hind legs as deadly weapons.

HABITAT Bison once roamed the grasslands of the Great Plains, where they were an important part of the Plains Indian culture. Today most bison are found on ranches or in game preserves where they are raised for their meat.

DIET Bison are herbivores, meaning they eat only plant material. Their diet includes grasses, herbs, shrubs, and twigs. Like cattle, bison store their food in a special stomach and then settle down to cough it up and chew it.

SURVIVAL In the 1800s, bison were hunted almost to extinction. By careful breeding and protection on ranches and preserves, the number of bison in North America is now about 200,000.

FACTS AT A GLANCE

RANGE Once found throughout the Great Plains of North America; now found on ranches and preserves

LIFE SPAN An average of 12 to 20 years in the wild

SIZE 900 to 2,200 pounds (408 to 998 kilograms)

DIET Grasses, herbs, shrubs, twigs

Despite their huge size, bison can change direction quickly and run at speeds up to 35 miles (56 kilometers) an hour.

AMERICAN BEAVERS

The American beaver is North America's largest rodent. Its webbed feet and broad, flat tail help it move through water very efficiently. The beaver has long, sharp teeth that it uses to cut down trees. Although gnawing on the tough wood of trees tends to wear down the beaver's teeth, the teeth are self-renewing—meaning that they continuously grow back. Beavers completely change the landscape in which they live. They build dams that create ponds as the surrounding forest is flooded. Then they build a den, called a lodge, with an underwater entrance for safety from predators. The average beaver colony is 6 to 7 animals, including parents and offspring of different ages.

Beavers are the real engineers of the animal kingdom. They use their sharp front teeth to cut down trees.

American beaver range

0   500 miles

0   500 kilometers

HABITAT American beavers live near ponds, marshes, rivers, and wetlands throughout North America. Beavers build dams and lodges using sticks, bark, mud, and logs that they have cut down themselves.

DIET Beavers eat aquatic plants such as pond weeds, water lilies, and cattails, as well as the soft inner bark of trees such as willows, aspens, maples, alders, and beeches.

SURVIVAL Beavers were once trapped for their valuable fur. They became almost extinct in the 1930s, but they are now protected and have again become common.

When swimming underwater beavers can close off their ears and nose. Their eyes are protected by a clear membrane.

FACTS AT A GLANCE

RANGE Ponds, marshes, rivers, and wetlands throughout North America

LIFE SPAN 20 years in the wild

SIZE 26 to 60 pounds (12 to 27 kilograms)

DIET Bark of trees, plus aquatic vegetation, buds, and roots

Beavers have two layers of fur—a top layer of coarse, long fur and an undercoat of fine, soft fur. The top coat is typically a dark reddish brown.

ANIMAL BITES

BEAVERS USE THEIR
FLAT TAIL FOR
**SLAPPING
THE SURFACE**
OF THE WATER TO
WARN OTHER BEAVERS
OF **DANGER.**

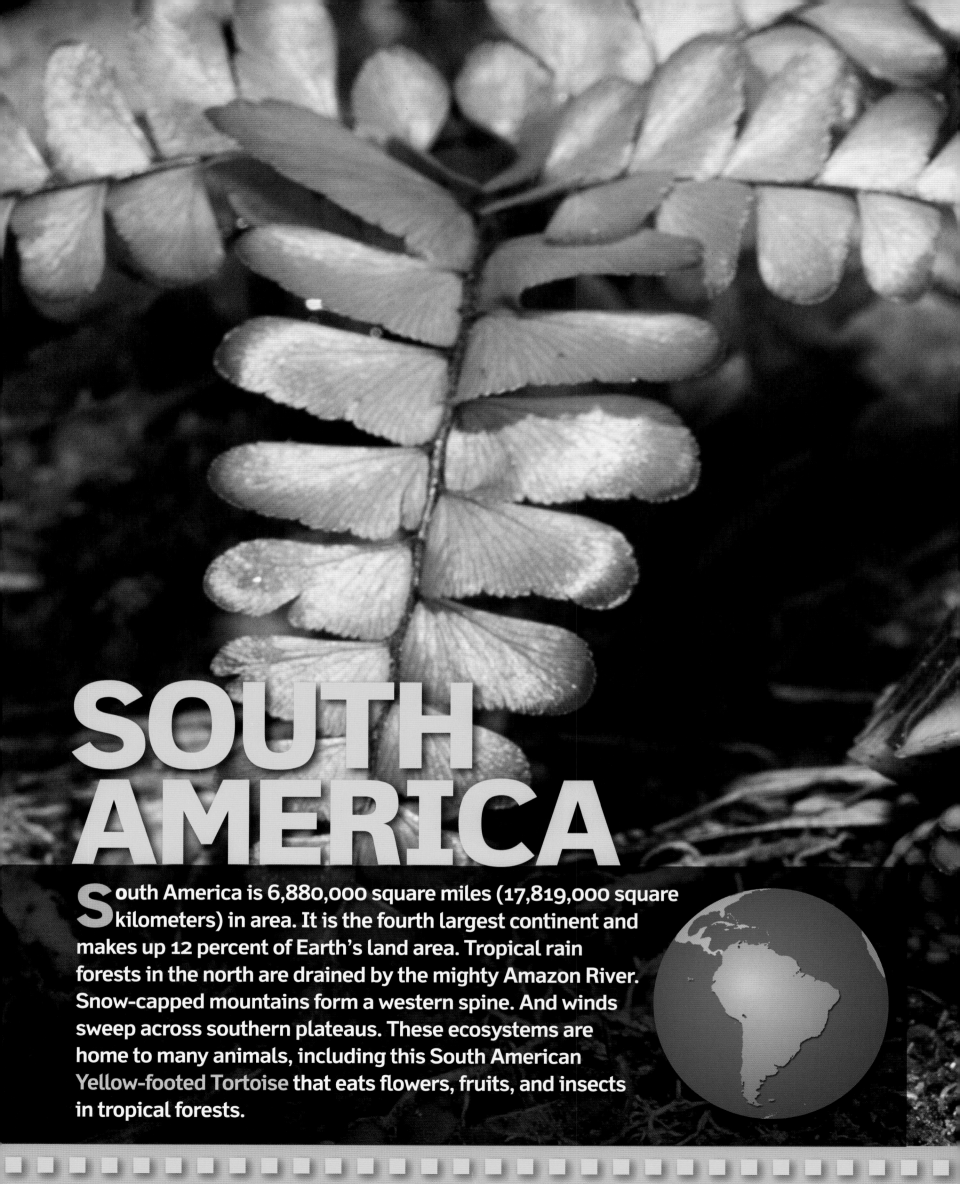

SOUTH AMERICA

South America is 6,880,000 square miles (17,819,000 square kilometers) in area. It is the fourth largest continent and makes up 12 percent of Earth's land area. Tropical rain forests in the north are drained by the mighty Amazon River. Snow-capped mountains form a western spine. And winds sweep across southern plateaus. These ecosystems are home to many animals, including this South American Yellow-footed Tortoise that eats flowers, fruits, and insects in tropical forests.

ANIMAL BITES

TORTOISES
HAVE LIVED ON **EARTH**
FOR ABOUT
**230 MILLION
YEARS,**
SINCE THE BEGINNING
OF THE AGE OF
THE DINOSAURS.

SOUTH AMERICA

South America is made up of many different ecosystems. Thousands of animals, birds, and fish live in the many environments—on the land, in the skies, or in the waters—of this continent.

DESERT The Lesser Rhea does not fly, but can run up to 37 miles (60 kilometers) per hour. These large birds live in herds of 5 to 30 individuals. They feed on plants and small animals.

MOUNTAIN Sure-footed Llamas are used by people in the Andes Mountains as pack animals on the rugged mountain terrain. Relatives of the camel, they are known to kick or even spit when tired.

FOREST Poison Dart Frogs, some of the most toxic animals on Earth, and bright colored butterflies, such as the Monarch, are just two of the species living in South America's rain forests. Scientists believe the vivid colors that make these creatures so beautiful may help scare away predators.

GRASSLAND Giant Anteaters use their tongues—more than 2 feet (0.6 meters) long—to catch insects. Anteaters live in grasslands and rain forests where they feast on as many as 35,000 ants and termites daily.

WETLAND The swamps and streams of this continent are home to the South American Tapir. A relative of the horse, tapirs use their trunk-like snouts to pull up grasses and aquatic plants.

Monarch Butterfly

Lesser Rhea

Giant Anteater

South American Tapir

Llama

Poison Dart Frog

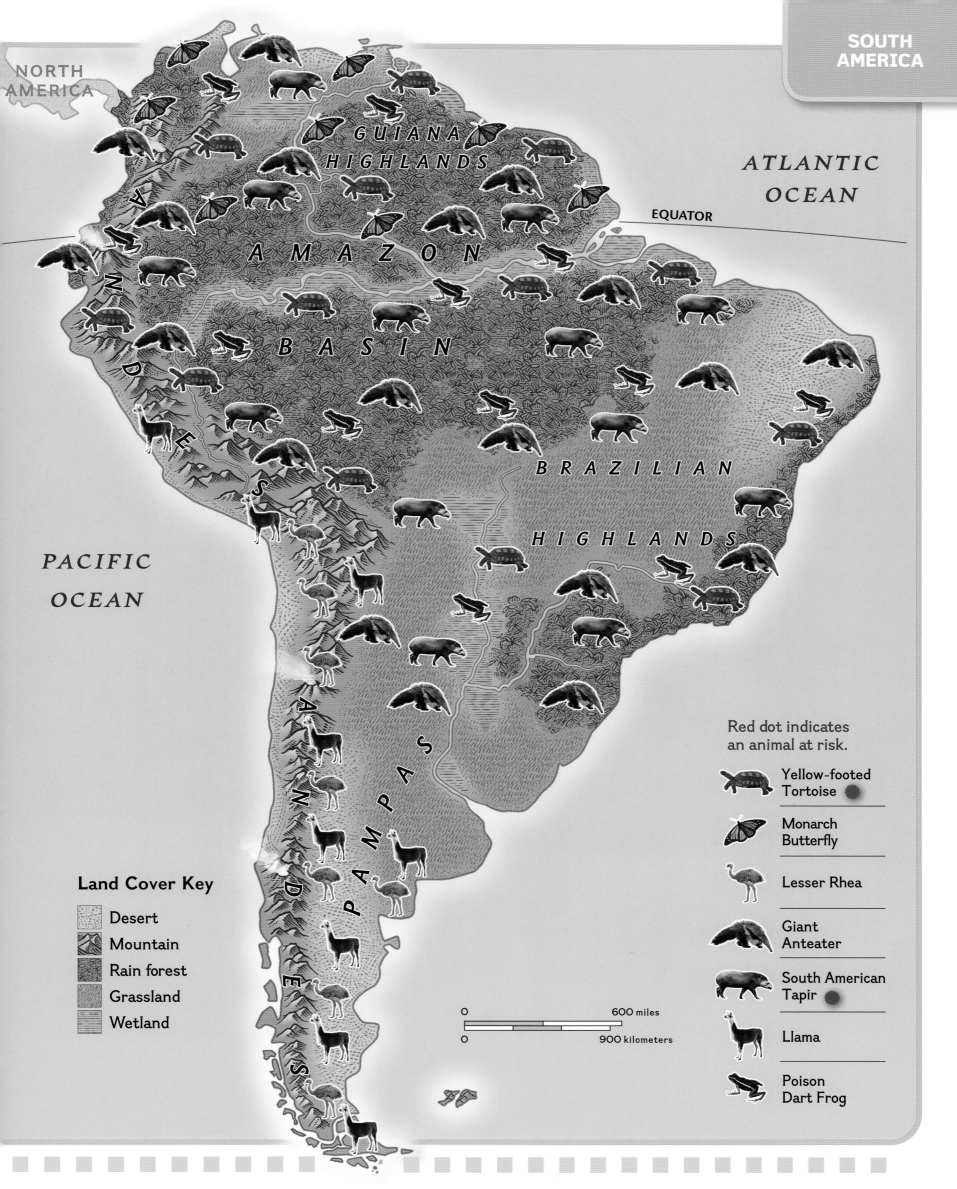

NORTH
AMERICA

GUIANA
HIGHLANDS

ATLANTIC
OCEAN

EQUATOR

A M A Z O N

B A S I N

A
N
D
E
S

PACIFIC
OCEAN

B R A Z I L I A N

H I G H L A N D S

P
A
M
P
A
S

A
N
D
E
S

Red dot indicates
an animal at risk.

Yellow-footed
Tortoise

Monarch
Butterfly

Lesser Rhea

Giant
Anteater

South American
Tapir

Llama

Poison
Dart Frog

Land Cover Key

Desert
Mountain
Rain forest
Grassland
Wetland

0   600 miles

0   900 kilometers

THE AMAZON RAIN FOREST

The Amazon River basin includes Earth's largest rain forest. The rain forest covers an area almost the size of the 48 contiguous United States. Cutting down trees has put many rain forest animals at risk. Here are some of the animals that live in the Amazon rain forest.

Amazon rain forest

ATLANTIC OCEAN

SOUTH AMERICA

0   1,000 miles
0   1,000 kilometers

Emergent layer
Up to 270 feet (82 m)

Canopy
65 to 130 feet
(20 to 40 m)

Understory
12 to 15 feet
(3 to 4 m)

Shrub layer

Forest floor

LAYERS OF THE AMAZON RAIN FOREST

Animal at risk

ANIMAL BITES

THE AMAZON RAIN FOREST PRODUCES ABOUT **20 PERCENT** OF EARTH'S **OXYGEN.**

GOLDEN LION TAMARIN
These small orange-yellow monkeys eat fruits, insects, and lizards. They are almost extinct in the wild.

GREEN ANACONDA
This powerful snake is the largest on Earth. It kills its prey by squeezing it to death.

SPOTTED JAGUAR
Jaguars are the third largest member of the cat family. They live near water in the dense forest.

BLUE-AND-YELLOW MACAW

This brilliant blue and yellow bird uses its strong beak to crack nuts and even coconuts.

THREE-TOED SLOTH

These sloths live in the treetops of the rain forest where they eat a diet of leaves and fruit.

PINK-TOED TARANTULA

Dark, hairy legs make this spider scary to look at, but its venom is weak and harmless to humans.

RED-BELLIED PIRANHA

This freshwater fish uses sharp teeth to consume meat. It does not aggressively attack humans, as sometimes reported.

CAIMAN

A member of the alligator family, caimans live in wetlands where they eat fish, reptiles, and birds.

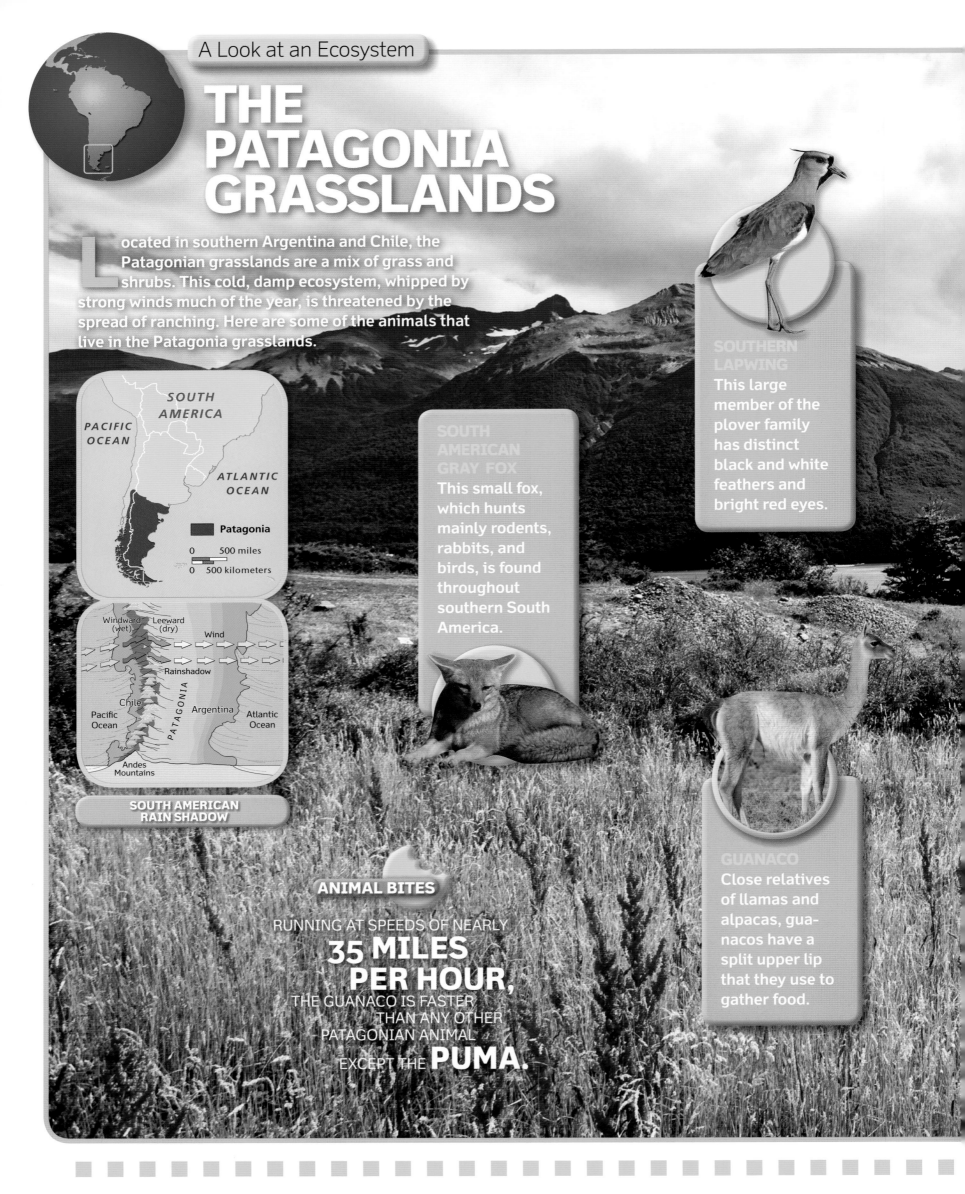

THE PATAGONIA GRASSLANDS

Located in southern Argentina and Chile, the Patagonian grasslands are a mix of grass and shrubs. This cold, damp ecosystem, whipped by strong winds much of the year, is threatened by the spread of ranching. Here are some of the animals that live in the Patagonia grasslands.

SOUTH AMERICA

PACIFIC OCEAN

ATLANTIC OCEAN

■ Patagonia

0   500 miles

0   500 kilometers

Windward (wet)   Leeward (dry)

Wind

Rainshadow

Chile

PATAGONIA

Pacific Ocean

Argentina

Atlantic Ocean

Andes Mountains

SOUTH AMERICAN RAIN SHADOW

SOUTHERN LAPWING

This large member of the plover family has distinct black and white feathers and bright red eyes.

SOUTH AMERICAN GRAY FOX

This small fox, which hunts mainly rodents, rabbits, and birds, is found throughout southern South America.

GUANACO

Close relatives of llamas and alpacas, guanacos have a split upper lip that they use to gather food.

ANIMAL BITES

RUNNING AT SPEEDS OF NEARLY

35 MILES PER HOUR,

THE GUANACO IS FASTER THAN ANY OTHER PATAGONIAN ANIMAL

EXCEPT THE **PUMA.**

DWARF ARMADILLO

This small armadillo lives in a shallow den that it digs in sandy soil with its sharp claws.

SOUTHERN CARACARA

These birds mate for life and are very territorial. They feed on fish, reptiles, eggs, and other birds.

GEOFFROY'S CAT

This cat, with its spotted and striped markings, was once hunted almost to extinction for its valuable pelt.

LESSER GRISON

This member of the ferret family eats a varied diet that includes small mammals, birds, eggs, and fruit.

PATAGONIAN HARE

This large relative of guinea pigs is the fourth largest rodent on Earth. It resembles a long-legged rabbit.

ANIMAL BITES

AT **2 WEEKS OLD**
A MONARCH BUTTERFLY
CATERPILLAR WEIGHS
**3,000
TIMES MORE**
THAN IT DID WHEN IT WAS BORN.

Spotlight on

BUTTERFLIES

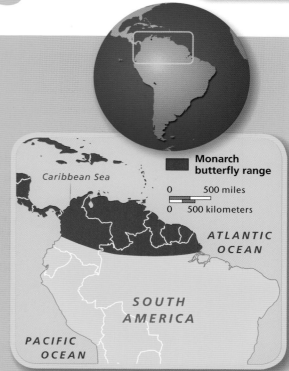

Monarch butterfly range

With their distinctive orange and black markings, monarchs are one of the most beautiful butterflies on Earth. In the butterfly stage, the northern and southern monarchs are almost identical.

The caterpillar, or larvae, stage lasts only about two weeks, during which the caterpillar does nothing but eat in order to grow and store energy.

There are two separate species of monarch butterflies. One is found in North America, while the other lives in South America. Scientists believe that these two species separated about two million years ago when world sea levels were much higher than they are today. The northern monarch migrates up to 2,500 miles (4,023 kilometers). In contrast, the southern monarch has a much shorter range. The lives of both species are marked by four distinct stages: egg, caterpillar (larvae), chrysalis (pupa), and adult butterfly.

HABITAT Monarch butterflies live where the milkweed plant is found because this plant plays an essential role in their breeding cycle. The southern monarch is found mainly between Argentina and the Amazon River, but the northern monarch migrates from North America to central Mexico and into northern South America. The southern monarch does not migrate over such long distances.

DIET During the caterpillar stage, monarchs eat milkweed, a plant that is poisonous to other animals. In the butterfly stage, they rely on nectar from flowers, liquid from fruits, and water. Monarchs use a small tube curled beneath their heads to suck up liquids.

SURVIVAL Loss of habitat is the greatest threat to monarch butterflies. For the northern monarch, deforestation in wintering areas in Mexico puts it at risk. Monarchs are also at risk from insecticides.

FACTS AT A GLANCE

RANGE Tropical and subtropical areas of South America

LIFE SPAN Adult butterflies live 4 to 5 weeks

SIZE Wingspan—4.3 inches (11 centimeters)

DIET Caterpillars eat milkweed plants; butterflies consume liquids

At two weeks, a caterpillar spins a cocoon, called a chrysalis. Over the next ten days, the caterpillar changes into a butterfly—a process called metamorphosis.

POISON DART FROGS

More than 300 different species of tree frogs live in Earth's tropical forests, but the greatest number are found in South America. They all have strong back legs that help them jump long distances. They also have a special sticky pad on the tip of each toe. This makes it possible for them to move about on the undersides of leaves without falling to the forest floor far below. Most other tree frogs are green, brown, or gray. This helps them blend into the foliage of the forest. But poison dart frogs have bright-colored markings that scientists believe may frighten away predators. Three species of poison dart frogs are poisonous to humans. One of Earth's deadliest venoms is found in their skin.

Poison dart frog range

0   500 miles
0   500 kilometers

Caribbean Sea

PACIFIC OCEAN

SOUTH AMERICA

ATLANTIC OCEAN

Poison dart frogs display a wide range of colors and markings, which may be a signal to predators to stay away.

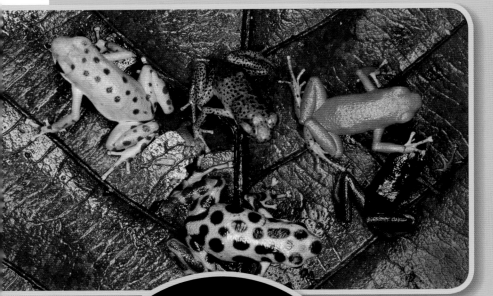

HABITAT Poison dart frogs are found in the tropics around the world. They live high above the forest floor among the leaves of tall rain forest trees.

DIET Most poison dart frogs hunt at night and live on a diet of bugs, flies, moths, and other small forest creatures. They catch their food with a fast flick of their long, sticky tongues.

SURVIVAL Most poison dart frogs are not endangered. However, as rain forests are cut down to make way for roads and agriculture, the habitat of poison dart frogs is shrinking. This may put these forest creatures at risk in the future.

Tadpoles develop inside a jelly-like mass of frog eggs on a leaf. After the tadpoles hatch, they mature into frogs.

FACTS AT A GLANCE

RANGE Among the leaves in the canopy of the rain forest in tropical regions around the world

LIFE SPAN 5 years in the wild

SIZE Average 3 inches (almost 8 centimeters)

DIET Crickets, flies, and other insects caught with a sticky tongue

Golden poison dart frogs range in color from bright yellow to pale green. Scientists are exploring ways to use the venom of these frogs to create a powerful painkiller.

ANIMAL BITES

THE **SKIN** OF A GOLDEN
POISON DART FROG
CONTAINS ENOUGH
TOXINS TO KILL
UP TO **20** PEOPLE.

ANIMAL BITES

Llamas make a
**HUMMING
NOISE**
and sometimes
HUM to their
OFFSPRING.

Spotlight on
LLAMAS

Llamas are intelligent, curious animals that are easily trained. Llamas are gentle and rarely bite or butt, but they will spit if they are overworked or feel threatened.

Llamas are one of the oldest domestic animals in the world. They were first bred for use as pack animals more than 4,000 years ago in the Andean Highlands of Peru. Llamas, like their relative the camel, have long necks and require very little water, but llamas do not have a hump. They quickly learn to wear a halter, carry heavy packs, and pull carts, but they cannot be ridden by humans.

SOUTH AMERICA

PACIFIC OCEAN

ATLANTIC OCEAN

Llama range

0   500 miles

0   500 kilometers

HABITAT Llamas are native to the high altiplano region of the Andes Mountains of South America. They and their close relatives—the alpaca, guanaco, and vicuña—are well adapted to the difficult mountainous terrain. Llamas have heavy pads on their feet that make them very sure-footed on steep, rocky mountain paths.

The coarse outer hair of the llama's coat is used to weave rugs; the soft undercoat is used to weave clothing and handicrafts.

DIET Llamas eat grasses, as well as twigs and branches from trees and shrubs. Like cows, they have more than one stomach. They store partially digested food in one stomach. Then later they chew this stored food, called cud, to complete the digestion process.

SURVIVAL Llamas are domesticated animals—meaning they are not found in the wild. It is estimated that the llama population in South America is at least 7 million, with another 100,000 animals on ranches in North America.

FACTS AT A GLANCE

RANGE Mountainous areas of South America

LIFE SPAN 15 to 25 years

SIZE 250 pounds (113 kilograms)

DIET Grasses, hay, and other plant material

Llama hair ranges in color from white to black, as well as many shades of brown. It may be solid or mixed.

EUROPE

Europe is 3,841,000 square miles (9,947,000 square kilometers) in area. It makes up almost 7 percent of Earth's land area. Only the continent of Australia is smaller. Europe is made up of many islands and peninsulas as well as broad plains and rugged mountains. These features provide the continent with diverse ecosystems. Among the many animals that call Europe home is this Eagle Owl, here soaring on silent wings at dusk.

ANIMAL BITES

EAGLE OWLS EAT
ALMOST **ANYTHING**
THEY CAN CATCH.
THEY HAVE BEEN KNOWN
TO EAT FOXES, DUCKS,
CRABS, SNAKES, AND
**EVEN OTHER
OWLS.**

EUROPE

The great variety of physical environments in Europe contributes to many different ecosystems. From the cold north to the warm Mediterranean shores, thousands of creatures live in these environments.

TUNDRA The Arctic Fox lives in the cold tundra, where temperatures fall below -50°F (-46°C) in winter. The fox uses its bushy tail to stay warm.

DESERT The Saiga Antelope has a light brown summer coat, but a white winter coat. Its unusual bulging nose filters the dusty summer air and warms the freezing winter air.

MOUNTAIN In summer, herds of Chamois graze in high alpine meadows, but in winter they migrate to lower elevations.

FOREST The Nightingale is a morning songbird that is common in the forests of Europe. But in the winter months it migrates to Africa.

GRASSLAND The Iberian Lynx is a relative of the North American bobcat. It is the most endangered member of the cat family. The remaining Iberian lynxes are found on the Iberian Peninsula.

WETLAND Eurasian Otters spend much of the time in freshwater streams and lakes in forest areas. They live in dens called holts and eat fish. They hunt mainly at night.

Chamois

Arctic Fox

Saiga Antelope

Nightingale

Eurasian Otter

Iberian Lynx

Iceland

ATLANTIC OCEAN

Norw

North Sea

Ireland

Great Britain

N O

A

Pyrenees

IBERIAN PENINSULA

Sardinia

M e d i

Red dot indicates an animal at risk.

Eagle Owl | Chamois | Arctic Fox | Saiga Antelope | Nightingale | Eurasian Otter | Iberian Lynx

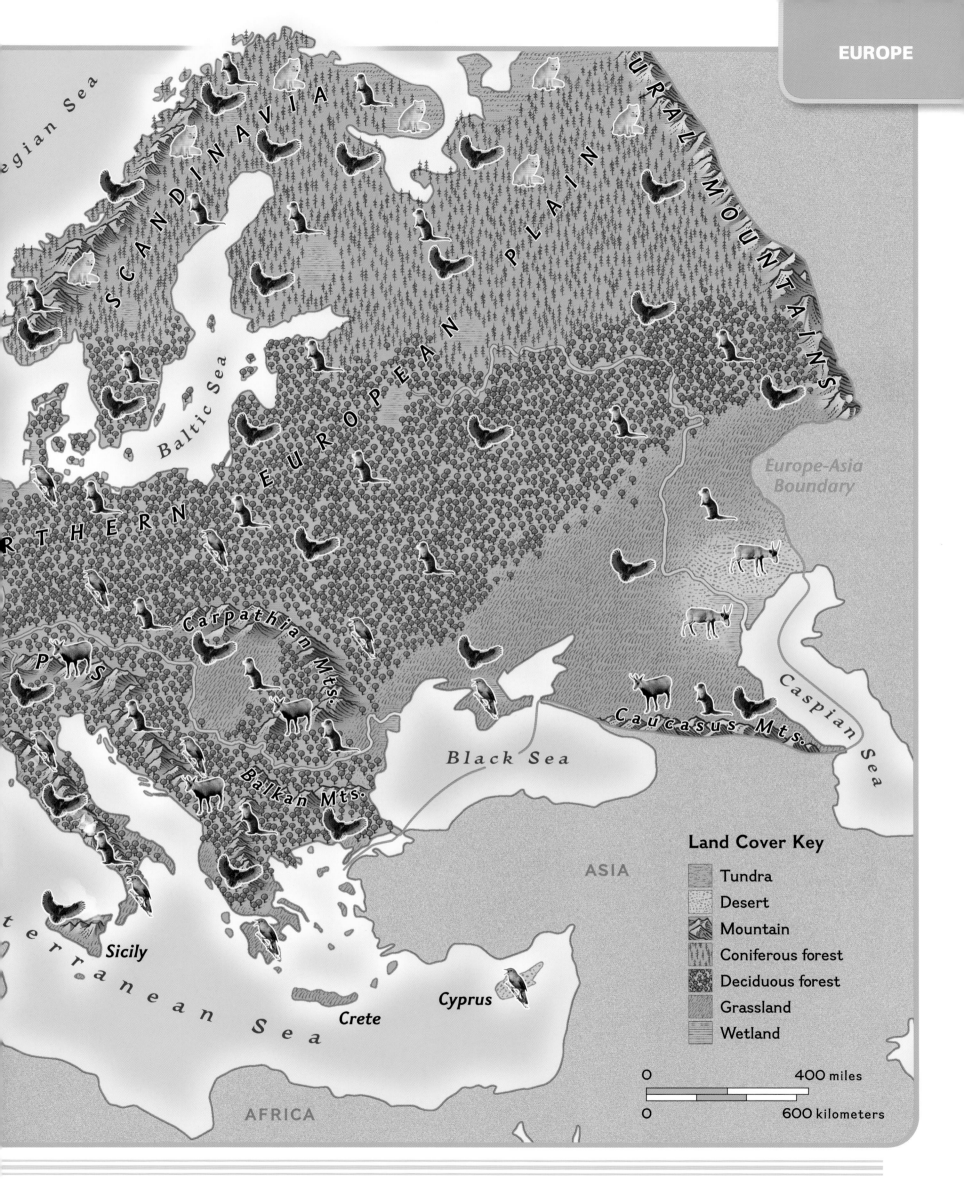

egian Sea

SCANDINAVIA

URAL MOUNTAINS

NORTHERN EUROPEAN PLAIN

Baltic Sea

Europe-Asia
Boundary

A L P S

Carpathian Mts.

Balkan Mts.

Caspian Sea

Caucasus Mts.

Black Sea

ASIA

Sicily

Sicily

terranean Sea

Cyprus

Crete

AFRICA

Land Cover Key

- Tundra
- Desert
- Mountain
- Coniferous forest
- Deciduous forest
- Grassland
- Wetland

0   400 miles

0   600 kilometers

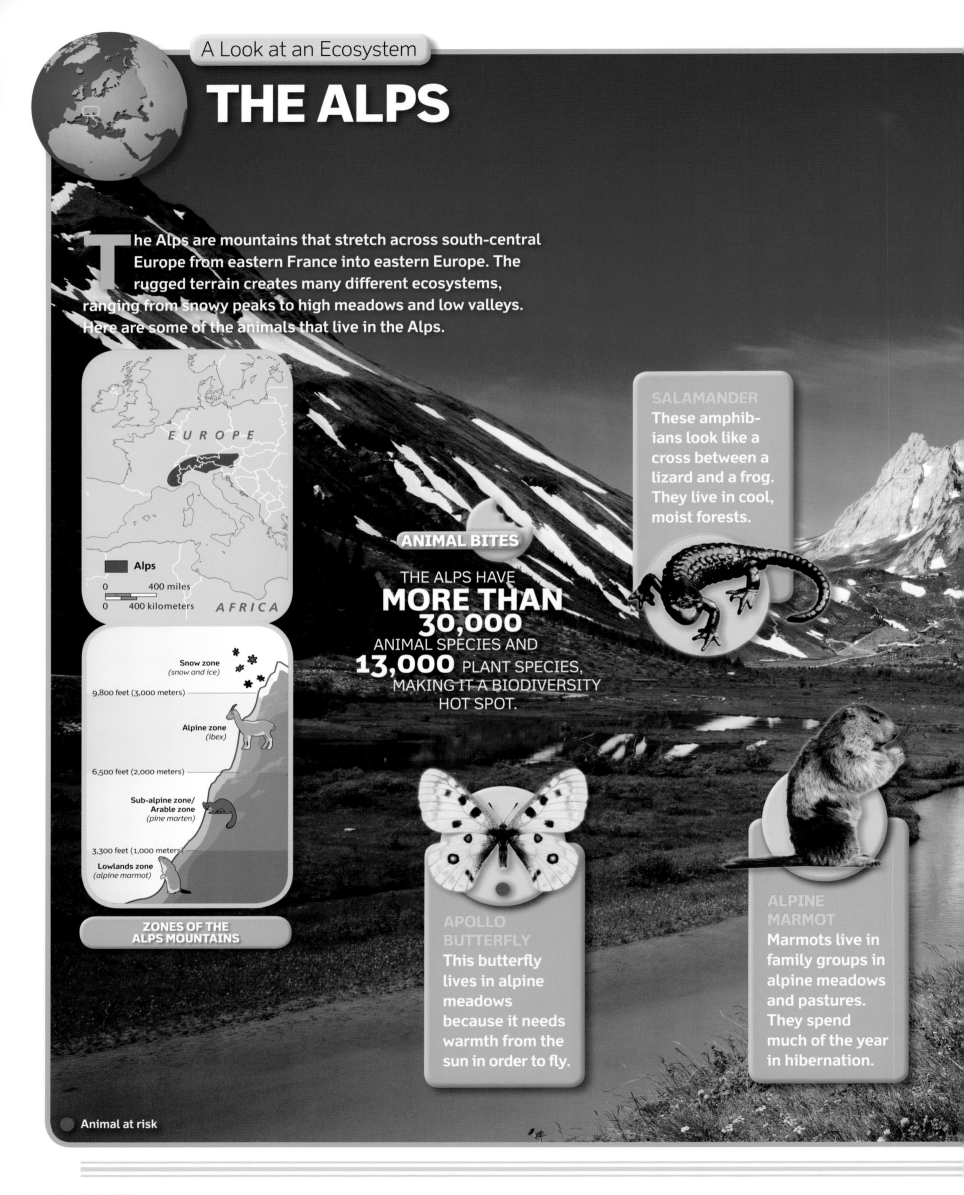

THE ALPS

The Alps are mountains that stretch across south-central Europe from eastern France into eastern Europe. The rugged terrain creates many different ecosystems, ranging from snowy peaks to high meadows and low valleys. Here are some of the animals that live in the Alps.

EUROPE

Alps

0 — 400 miles
0 — 400 kilometers

AFRICA

Snow zone
(snow and ice)

9,800 feet (3,000 meters)

Alpine zone
(ibex)

6,500 feet (2,000 meters)

Sub-alpine zone/
Arable zone
(pine marten)

3,300 feet (1,000 meters)

Lowlands zone
(alpine marmot)

**ZONES OF THE
ALPS MOUNTAINS**

ANIMAL BITES

THE ALPS HAVE
MORE THAN
30,000
ANIMAL SPECIES AND
13,000 PLANT SPECIES,
MAKING IT A BIODIVERSITY
HOT SPOT.

SALAMANDER
These amphibians look like a cross between a lizard and a frog. They live in cool, moist forests.

APOLLO BUTTERFLY
This butterfly lives in alpine meadows because it needs warmth from the sun in order to fly.

ALPINE MARMOT
Marmots live in family groups in alpine meadows and pastures. They spend much of the year in hibernation.

Animal at risk

GOLDEN EAGLE
This large bird soars on updrafts in mountainous terrain. It uses sharp talons to catch small mammals.

ALPINE IBEX
The male ibex has long curved horns; the female's horns are short. Ibex live on rugged mountain slopes.

ROCK PTARMIGAN
This bird lives on rocky mountain slopes. Its feathers change from white in winter to brown in summer.

CAPERCAILLIE
These birds are clumsy fliers because of their short wings and heavy bodies. They eat mainly berries.

PINE MARTIN
This member of the weasel family is about the size of a cat. Its main food is mice.

THE EUROPEAN TUNDRA

The tundra is Europe's northernmost and coldest ecosystem. Although covered with snow much of the year, the tundra comes to life with small shrubs, mosses, and grasses during the short summer when temperatures may reach 34 to 57°F (3 to 12°C). Here are some of the animals that live in the European tundra.

ANIMAL BITES

THE ARCTIC TUNDRA HAS **24 HOURS** OF SUNLIGHT IN **SUMMER** AND 24 HOURS OF DARKNESS IN **WINTER.**

Greenland

ARCTIC OCEAN

ASIA

EUROPE

■ Tundra

0 — 500 miles
0 — 500 kilometers

AMOUNT OF RAINFALL IN DIFFERENT BIOMES

90"

60"

30"

10"*

10"

| Desert | Grassland | Rainforest | Temperate Deciduous Forest | Tundra |

* Inches of rainfall per year

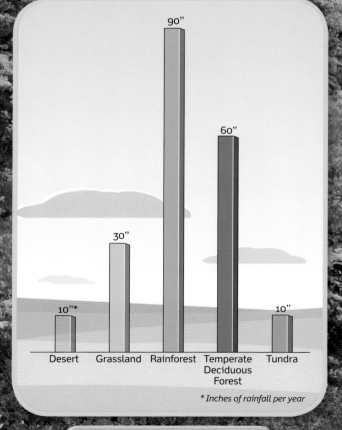

WOLVERINE
This largest member of the weasel family is a fierce predator, hunting rabbits, rodents, and occasionally even caribou.

ERMINE
This fast-moving animal feeds mainly on small mammals. Its fur is white in winter but brown in summer.

SNOWY OWL
White feathers offer this bird perfect camouflage in the Arctic environment where its favorite food is lemmings.

TUNDRA SWAN
This large bird lays 3 to 5 eggs in a nest lined with down that it builds on the tundra.

ARCTIC SKUA
These aggressive seabirds steal much of their food from other birds. Skuas come ashore only to breed.

MUSK OX
A long shaggy coat keeps musk oxen warm during Arctic winters. Living in herds offers protection against predators.

NORWAY LEMMING
These small mammals search for food day and night, even digging tunnels under the snow in winter.

BROWN BEAR
Despite their size, these large bears have been clocked at speeds of 30 miles (48 kilometers) per hour.

ARCTIC FOXES

Arctic foxes have adapted to survive in tundra regions where winter temperatures may reach as low as -58°F (-50°C). During the winter, the foxes have long white fur that keeps them warm. But the color of their fur also helps protect them from other animals because it blends into the snowy landscape. In summer, as the snow melts, the foxes shed their white winter coat and grow shorter brownish-gray fur that blends into the summer landscape of the tundra.

Arctic fox pups develop their hunting skills by playing games of attack with each other. They begin to hunt as early as three months old.

HABITAT Arctic foxes live in the bitterly cold coastal margins around the Arctic Ocean. They build dens, mostly facing south to catch the warm rays of the low Arctic sun, in mounds of dirt or in rocky cliffs. But in winter they may burrow into the snow for shelter.

DIET Arctic foxes are omnivores—meaning they eat a diet that includes both meat and plant material. They prefer small mammals, but also eat birds, insects, berries, and eggs. They even eat the remains of animals killed by larger animals.

SURVIVAL Arctic foxes are found widely in northern areas of Europe, Asia, and North America. They are sometimes hunted by native people for their thick white winter fur, but they are not considered endangered.

An Arctic fox pup stretches as it emerges from its den. An average litter includes seven pups that are fully weaned by six weeks of age.

FACTS AT A GLANCE

RANGE Treeless tundra areas near the Arctic coasts of Europe, Asia, and North America

LIFE SPAN 3 to 6 years in the wild

SIZE 6.5 to 17 pounds (3 to 8 kilograms)

DIET Small mammals, birds, berries, and eggs

The white coat of the Arctic fox blends into the snowy winter landscape. Arctic foxes usually mate for life. The male helps the female, called a vixen, raise the pups.

ANIMAL BITES

AN ARCTIC FOX'S DEN
IS MADE UP OF
A **NETWORK
OF TUNNELS,**
OFTEN UNDERGROUND
AND WITH **MULTIPLE
ENTRANCES.**

ANIMAL BITES

OTTERS ARE
VERY **PLAYFUL.**
SOMETIMES THEY
PLAY "TAG,"
SLIDE DOWN **MUD** BANKS,
OR SLIP AND SLIDE IN THE
SNOW.

EURASIAN OTTERS

Otters, with their webbed feet, are excellent swimmers and spend a lot of time in water.

Otters are sometimes referred to as the clowns of the animal kingdom because of their playful antics on land and in the water. The Eurasian otter has short legs and a long body that is covered with thick brown fur. Each webbed paw has five toes that help make the otter an excellent swimmer. Otters typically have two to three cubs in a litter. The cubs stay with their mother until they are about one year old.

HABITAT The Eurasian otter is the most widespread member of the otter family. Otters live in freshwater streams and ponds as well as in coastal areas. Otters dig burrows called holts in the banks of rivers. They are found throughout Europe, and also in Asia and North Africa.

Otters have thick fur that makes them well-adapted to cold winters. They even seem to enjoy playing in the snow.

DIET The Eurasian otter, like its cousins around the world, lives on a diet made up mainly of fish. But it also eats other aquatic life, as well as small birds, insects, and frogs. In fact, otters will eat almost anything they can hold. Their diet tends to vary depending on what is readily available.

SURVIVAL Eurasian otters are at risk from humans, large birds of prey, such as eagles and falcons, and large meat-eating animals, such as lynxes and wolves. Humans also hunt them for their fur.

Eurasian otter range

0   500 miles
0   500 kilometers

FACTS AT A GLANCE

RANGE Freshwater streams and coastal areas throughout Europe, Asia, and North Africa

LIFE SPAN Up to 22 years in captivity

SIZE 15 to 22 pounds (7 to 10 kilograms)

DIET Mainly fish, but also other aquatic life, including amphibians

These young otters appear curious about their environment. When otters are about ten weeks old, they venture out of the nest.

NIGHTINGALES

Nightingales received their name because, unlike many other birds, their song can be heard at night as well as during the daytime. The males are the singers, and it is thought that they sing to attract a mate or to protect their territory. Both males and females are brown in color, with a reddish tail and a creamy underside. Nightingales mate in the springtime, and the female builds a cup-shaped nest made of twigs, leaves, and grass near the ground in dense bushes. Nightingales have long been mentioned in literature, dating all the way back to the Greek poet Homer's epic poem *The Odyssey.* English poet John Keats also wrote of the bird in his famous "Ode to a Nightingale."

The nightingale's song includes many different sounds. The male bird, unlike most other birds, sings his song at night as well as during the day.

HABITAT Nightingales live at lower elevations in areas of forest and dry woodland throughout southern areas of Europe and Southwest Asia. Nightingales migrate to North Africa during the cold winter season.

DIET Nightingales are omnivorous birds—meaning they eat a varied diet that includes insects, as well as fruits, seeds, and nuts.

SURVIVAL Nightingales are widespread across Europe. They have many natural predators, including rats, foxes, cats, and reptiles, but they are not considered endangered.

FACTS AT A GLANCE

RANGE Forests and dry woodland areas of Europe and Southwest Asia; winter migrations to North Africa

LIFE SPAN 1 to 3 years in the wild

SIZE 6 to 6.5 inches (15 to 16.5 centimeters)

DIET Insects, fruits, seeds, and nuts

Baby nightingales, with their mouths wide open, wait for a lunch of insects. The female nightingale lays two to five eggs that hatch after about two weeks.

Although the nightingale's loud song is easily heard, the bird itself, with its brown feathers, can be difficult to spot in the dense foliage that it favors.

Nightingale range

0   500 miles
0   500 kilometers

EUROPE

AFRICA

ASIA

ANIMAL BITES

NIGHTINGALES SOMETIMES
**NEST ON THE
GROUND**
NEAR DENSE BUSHES.
THEY MIGRATE SOUTH
AND SPEND
**WINTERS
IN AFRICA.**

TIGERS CAN EAT
40 POUNDS
(18 KILOGRAMS)
IN A SINGLE SITTING.
AFTER A BIG MEAL,
THEY CAN GO UP TO
ONE WEEK
WITHOUT EATING.

ASIA

Asia is 17,208,000 square miles (44,570,000 square kilometers) in area. It is the largest of all the continents and makes up 30 percent of Earth's land area. Asia stretches all the way from the icy shores of the Arctic Ocean to the waters of the Indian and Pacific Oceans. Its many ecosystems range from mountains to tropical forests and deserts, with an equally broad range of animals, including the majestic but endangered Bengal Tiger.

ASIA

Asia's vast expanse includes many ecosystems, ranging from cold to hot, and wet to dry. Many different animals, birds, and fish live on the land, in the skies, or in the waters of this continent.

TUNDRA Caribou are members of the deer family. Unlike other deer, both males and females have antlers. Caribou migrate hundreds of miles in search of food and use their large hooves to dig through the snow for food during the long winters.

DESERT Bactrian Camels live in the rocky deserts of Central Asia. They rely on fat stored in two humps on their back when water and food are not available.

MOUNTAIN Yaks live at elevations up to 19,000 feet (5,791 meters) in the mountains and plateaus of Tibet. Their broad hooves and heavy, woolly coat are adaptations to the extremes of the mountain environment.

FOREST Giant Pandas live in forests with a dense understory of bamboo, their favorite food. Pandas are endangered, with fewer than 2,000 remaining in the wild.

GRASSLAND Unlike its African relative, the Greater One-horned Asian Rhinoceros has just one horn. Its diet is mainly grasses, leaves, and fruits. This rhino is endangered, with only about 2,000 remaining in the wild.

WETLAND The Fishing Cat lives near marshes and streams where it hunts birds, small mammals, snakes, and fish. It dives into the water and uses partially webbed paws to catch prey.

Caribou

Bactrian Camel

Yak

Fishing Cat

Giant Panda

Greater One-horned Asian Rhinoceros

EUROPE

Mediterranean Sea

Black Sea

Europe-Asia Boundary

THE

Caspian Sea

AFRICA

Red Sea

ARABIAN PENINSULA

Arabian Sea

INDIAN

BLACK-CROWNED NIGHT HERON
This bird has a black cap, yellow legs, and red eyes. It has a shorter bill than other herons.

BLUE-EARED KINGFISHER
This small bird, with bright blue feathers, catches fish in pools and streams in the tropical forests.

OLIVE RIDLEY TURTLE
This small sea turtle gets its name from the color of its heart-shaped shell, called a carapace.

GANGES RIVER DOLPHIN
This animal's eyes have no lenses, so it is blind. It is endangered because of pollution in the delta.

INDIAN PYTHON
This snake kills its prey by squeezing it. It may eat only once a year.

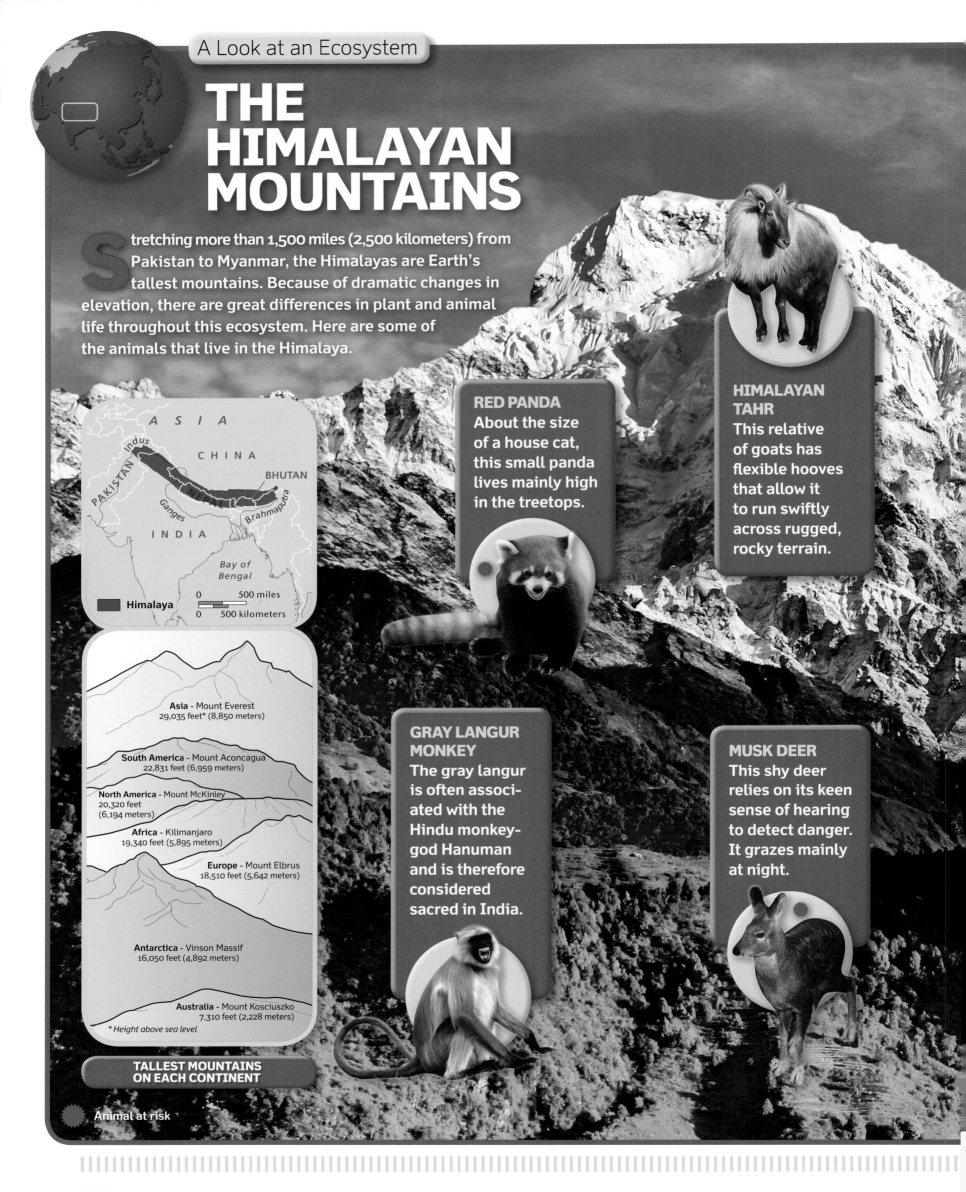

THE HIMALAYAN MOUNTAINS

Stretching more than 1,500 miles (2,500 kilometers) from Pakistan to Myanmar, the Himalayas are Earth's tallest mountains. Because of dramatic changes in elevation, there are great differences in plant and animal life throughout this ecosystem. Here are some of the animals that live in the Himalaya.

ASIA

Indus

CHINA

PAKISTAN

BHUTAN

NEPAL

Ganges

Brahmaputra

INDIA

Bay of Bengal

■ Himalaya

0   500 miles

0   500 kilometers

Asia - Mount Everest
29,035 feet* (8,850 meters)

South America - Mount Aconcagua
22,831 feet (6,959 meters)

North America - Mount McKinley
20,320 feet
(6,194 meters)

Africa - Kilimanjaro
19,340 feet (5,895 meters)

Europe - Mount Elbrus
18,510 feet (5,642 meters)

Antarctica - Vinson Massif
16,050 feet (4,892 meters)

Australia - Mount Kosciuszko
7,310 feet (2,228 meters)

* Height above sea level

TALLEST MOUNTAINS ON EACH CONTINENT

● Animal at risk

RED PANDA
About the size of a house cat, this small panda lives mainly high in the treetops.

HIMALAYAN TAHR
This relative of goats has flexible hooves that allow it to run swiftly across rugged, rocky terrain.

GRAY LANGUR MONKEY
The gray langur is often associated with the Hindu monkey-god Hanuman and is therefore considered sacred in India.

MUSK DEER
This shy deer relies on its keen sense of hearing to detect danger. It grazes mainly at night.

HIMALAYAN MONAL
This brightly colored pheasant prefers the cool temperatures of high elevations. Its diet includes roots and insects.

GOLDEN EAGLE
This bird dives at speeds of more than 150 miles (241 kilometers) per hour to catch its prey.

ASIAN BLACK BEAR
These bears are active during the day and sleep at night. They become nocturnal around humans.

ASIAN ELEPHANT
Although smaller than its African cousin, this elephant eats up to 300 pounds (136 kilograms) of food daily.

ANIMAL BITES

THE **HIMALAYAN RANGE** IS HOME TO **30** OF THE WORLD'S HIGHEST **MOUNTAINS.**

ANIMAL BITES

A RHINO'S HEAD
CAN WEIGH
800 TO 1,000
POUNDS
(362 TO 464 KILOGRAMS).

RHINOCEROSES

⬅ *Illegal hunting has put greater one-horned rhinoceroses at risk. They are hunted for their horns, which are believed to have important medicinal value.*

⬇ *Adult females generally live alone except when they have a calf. Mother rhinoceroses often remain with their calves for up to four years.*

The greater one-horned Asian rhinoceros, often referred to as the Indian rhinoceros, is built somewhat like a tank. Its thick leathery hide is brownish-gray with folds that look like plates of armor. As its name suggests, it has a single horn, 8 to 24 inches (20 to 61 centimeters) long and black in color, made of material similar to human fingernails. Rhinoceroses have very good senses of hearing and smell, but their eyesight is extremely poor.

HABITAT Greater one-horned Asian rhinoceroses live in moist grasslands, swamps, and nearby forests where they can find an abundance of grass. They also spend a lot of time submerged in water or wallowing in wet mud to keep off biting flies.

DIET Greater one-horned Asian rhinoceroses are strict vegetarians. Their main food is grass, but they will also eat leaves, branches, aquatic plants, and fruit. When food supplies become limited, these huge animals have been known to consume field crops and pasture as well.

SURVIVAL Greater one-horned Asian rhinoceroses once ranged from Pakistan across northern India and Nepal, to the border of Myanmar. But today they have been hunted almost to extinction. About 2,000 animals remain in protected areas in India and Nepal.

ASIA

HIMALAYA
NEPAL BHUTAN
INDIA

■ Greater one-horned Asian rhinoceros range

0 — 500 miles
0 — 500 kilometers

FACTS AT A GLANCE

RANGE Grassland and adjacent forests, mainly in protected parks in India and Nepal

LIFE SPAN About 40 years in captivity

SIZE 4,000 to 6,000 pounds (1,800 to 2,700 kilograms)

DIET Grasses, leaves, branches, and fruit

⬅ *The greater one-horned Asian rhinoceros has a semi-prehensile upper lip. This means it can use its upper lip to grasp grass as it eats.*

GIANT PANDAS

Like most other bears, giant pandas are very agile. They are skilled tree-climbers and use their paws to grasp trunks as they climb.

Black-and-white giant pandas are considered a national treasure in China. Giant pandas have appeared in Chinese paintings for thousands of years. They are also a favorite animal in zoos around the world. Giant pandas are relatives of bears. They are similar to bears in the way they walk and climb. And like other bears, they can be quite dangerous. Panda cubs are born blind and weigh just 5 ounces (142 grams). They are born without any hair and develop their black-and-white coloring as they mature. Adult giant pandas spend up to 12 hours each day feeding. Unlike many other bears, pandas do not hibernate.

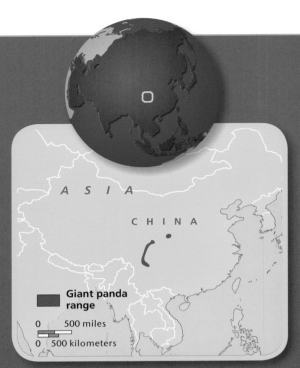

ASIA

CHINA

Giant panda range

0   500 miles

0   500 kilometers

HABITAT Giant pandas living in the wild are found at elevations ranging from 5,000 to 10,000 feet (1,524 to 3,048 meters) in cold, rainy broadleaf and coniferous forests that have a dense undergrowth of bamboo.

DIET In the wild, giant pandas live on a diet of bamboo. They have large molars and strong jaws that enable them to crush the tough, woody bamboo. In zoos, they also eat sugarcane, apples, and sweet potatoes.

SURVIVAL Giant pandas are endangered due to loss of habitat and shortages of bamboo. There are about 1,600 pandas remaining in the wild and another 160 living in zoos.

Giant pandas have an extra wrist bone called a "panda's thumb" that helps them hold and eat bamboo.

FACTS AT A GLANCE

RANGE In misty bamboo and evergreen forests of central China, elevations above 5,000 feet (1,524 meters)

LIFE SPAN 20 years in the wild

SIZE Up to 300 pounds (136 kilograms)

DIET 99 percent bamboo

A mother panda gently cuddles her baby. At birth a panda cub is helpless. It may stay with its mother up to three years.

ANIMAL BITES

PANDAS MAKE A **BLEATING** SOUND SIMILAR TO A LAMB OR A GOAT KID. IT'S A **FRIENDLY** NOISE THEY USE TO GREET EACH OTHER.

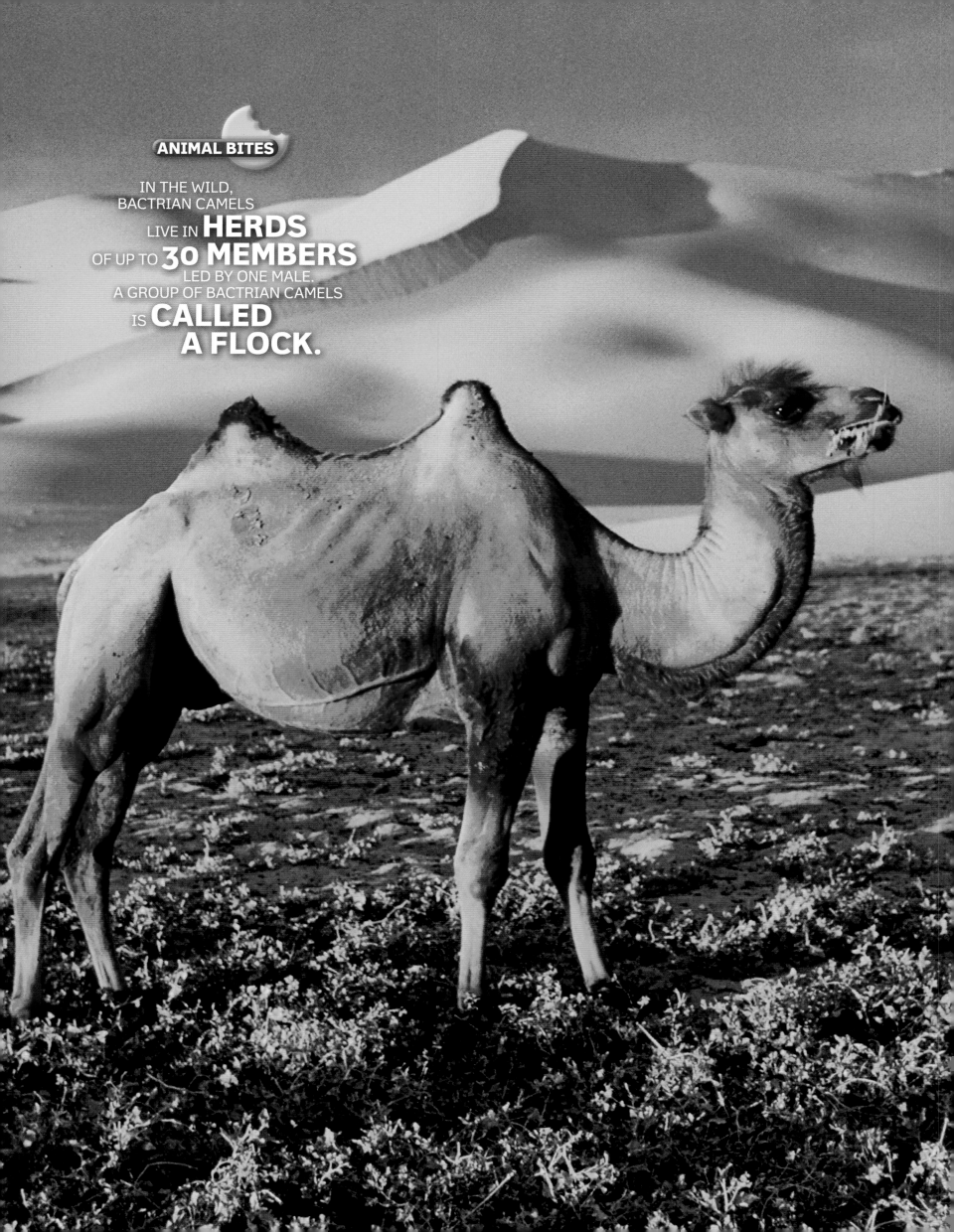

ANIMAL BITES

IN THE WILD,
BACTRIAN CAMELS
LIVE IN **HERDS**
OF UP TO **30 MEMBERS**
LED BY ONE MALE.
A GROUP OF BACTRIAN CAMELS
IS **CALLED
A FLOCK.**

BACTRIAN CAMELS

The only truly wild camels that remain are Bactrian camels living in the Gobi desert of Mongolia and China. These wild herds number fewer than 1,000 animals in total.

Bactrian camels have two humps, unlike the Arabian camel, which has only one. But whether one or two, the humps are made up of stored fat that help the camels go for long periods without water. When water is not available, the fat is converted to water and energy. However, when there is water, a thirsty camel can drink up to 30 gallons (114 liters) in as little as 10 minutes. Camels have been used for generations as pack animals. They are able to carry 375 to 600 pounds (170 to 270 kilograms) up to 30 miles (48 kilometers) a day.

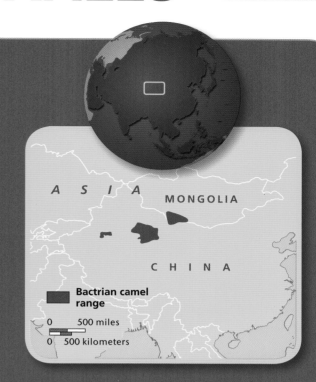

Bactrian camel range

0   500 miles
0   500 kilometers

The Bactrian camel is able to close its nostrils against blowing sand, while bushy eyebrows and a double row of eyelashes protect its eyes.

HABITAT Wild Bactrian camels live in the extreme environment of the rocky Gobi desert of Mongolia and China. In the summer, temperatures can rise above 100°F (38°C). But in the winter the temperature can fall to -20°F (-28°C). The camel's long shaggy coat keeps it warm in winter, but it quickly sheds this long hair as summer approaches.

DIET The Bactrian camel prefers grasses, leaves, and shrubs, but it is also able to digest thorns and other dry vegetation when better food is not available.

SURVIVAL Domesticated camels number as many as two million, but wild Bactrian camels are considered endangered due to loss of habitat.

FACTS AT A GLANCE

RANGE Rocky deserts of Central and East Asia

LIFE SPAN Up to 50 years

SIZE Over 7 feet (2 meters) at the hump

DIET Leaves, grasses, and shrubs

A baby camel is able to stand and run a few hours after birth. It stays with its mother for three to five years.

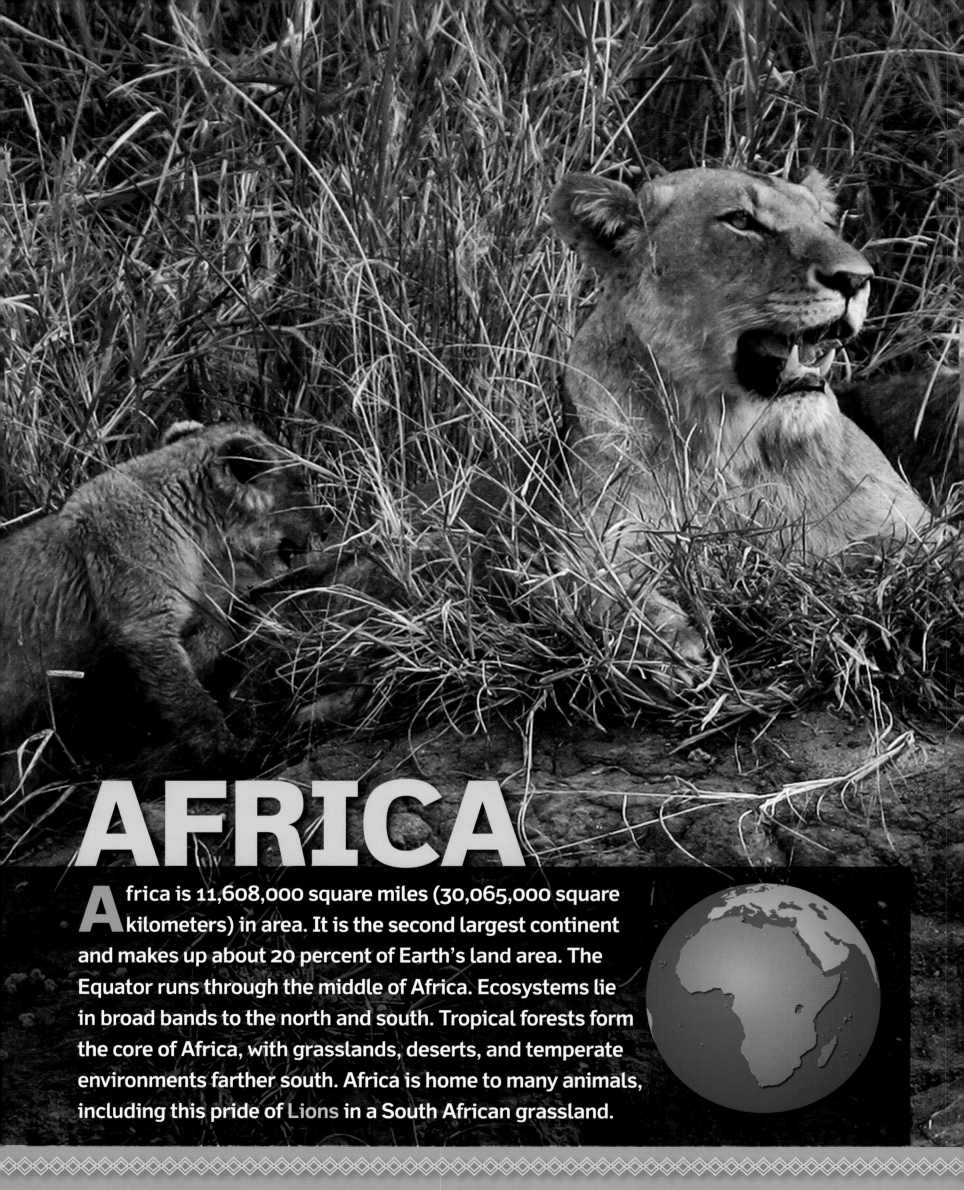

AFRICA

Africa is 11,608,000 square miles (30,065,000 square kilometers) in area. It is the second largest continent and makes up about 20 percent of Earth's land area. The Equator runs through the middle of Africa. Ecosystems lie in broad bands to the north and south. Tropical forests form the core of Africa, with grasslands, deserts, and temperate environments farther south. Africa is home to many animals, including this pride of Lions in a South African grassland.

ANIMAL BITES

A MOTHER LION
TAKES CARE OF HER
MALE CUBS FOR
ABOUT **TWO YEARS,**
BUT **FEMALE** CUBS MAY
LIVE WITH THEIR MOTHER
FOR **LIFE.**

AFRICA

Cheetah

Gorilla

Zebra

Hippopotamus

Spiny-tailed Lizard

Chimpanzee

Africa includes many different ecosystems, but it has no extremely cold environments. The continent is a rich blend of mammals, birds, and fish living in different environments on the land, in the air, or in the water.

DESERT The Spiny-tailed Lizard is a desert dweller. It tolerates hot days and chilly nights. It eats leaves, seeds, and insects, but requires very little water. Some varieties reach 30 inches (76 centimeters) in length.

MOUNTAIN Gorillas live near the Equator on mountain slopes and in bamboo forests, as well as in lowland rain forests. They live in groups called troops, led by a large male called a "silverback."

FOREST Chimpanzees live in social communities of several dozen animals in the rain forests and woodlands of central and western Africa. Among all creatures of the animal kingdom, they are the most closely related to humans.

GRASSLAND Many animals associated with Africa, such as Zebras and Cheetahs, are found in tropical grasslands called savannas. Zebras are grass eaters. But cheetahs are meat eaters that hunt other grassland animals for their food.

WETLAND The Hippopotamus lives in rivers and lakes of Africa. On land it can outrun the fastest human, at least for a short distance. Hippos spend their days in the water, but come out at night to graze on land.

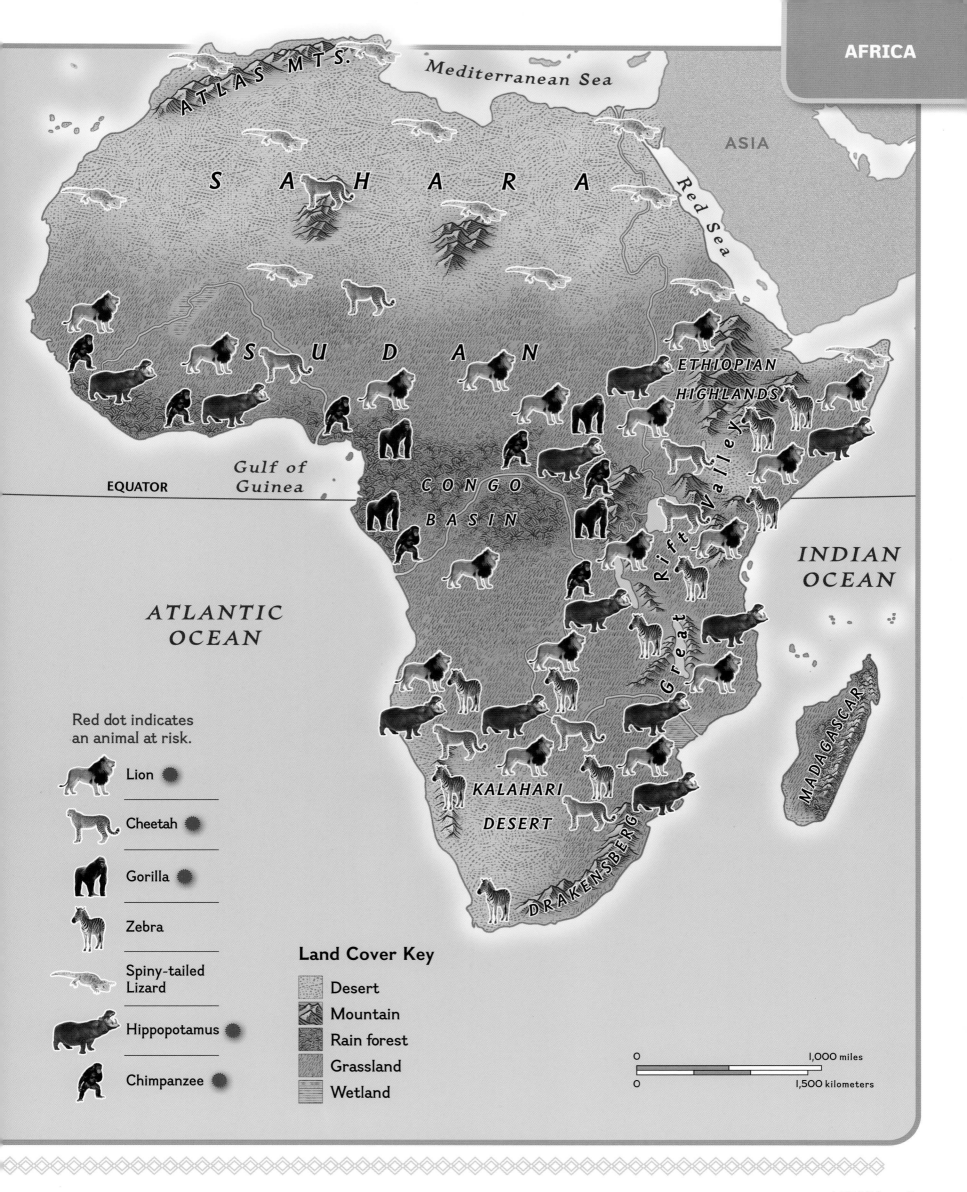

ATLAS MTS.

Mediterranean Sea

ASIA

S A H A R A

Red Sea

S U D A N

ETHIOPIAN
HIGHLANDS

Gulf of
Guinea

EQUATOR

C O N G O
B A S I N

Great Rift Valley

INDIAN
OCEAN

ATLANTIC
OCEAN

MADAGASCAR

KALAHARI

DESERT

DRAKENSBERG

Red dot indicates
an animal at risk.

Lion ●

Cheetah ●

Gorilla ●

Zebra

Spiny-tailed
Lizard

Hippopotamus ●

Chimpanzee ●

Land Cover Key

Desert

Mountain

Rain forest

Grassland

Wetland

0   1,000 miles

0   1,500 kilometers

THE SAVANNA

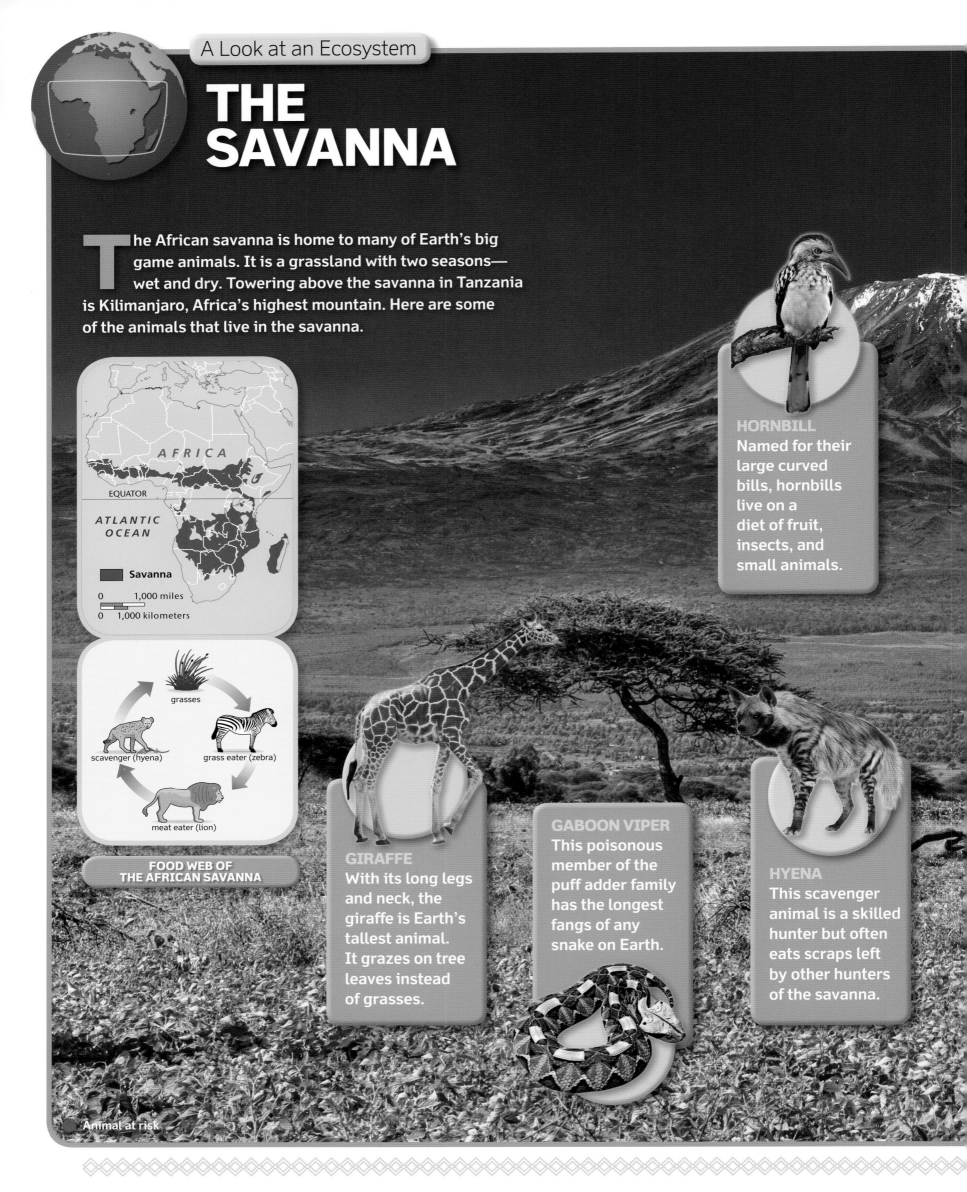

The African savanna is home to many of Earth's big game animals. It is a grassland with two seasons—wet and dry. Towering above the savanna in Tanzania is Kilimanjaro, Africa's highest mountain. Here are some of the animals that live in the savanna.

AFRICA

EQUATOR

ATLANTIC OCEAN

■ Savanna

0 — 1,000 miles
0 — 1,000 kilometers

grasses

scavenger (hyena)

grass eater (zebra)

meat eater (lion)

FOOD WEB OF THE AFRICAN SAVANNA

HORNBILL
Named for their large curved bills, hornbills live on a diet of fruit, insects, and small animals.

GIRAFFE
With its long legs and neck, the giraffe is Earth's tallest animal. It grazes on tree leaves instead of grasses.

GABOON VIPER
This poisonous member of the puff adder family has the longest fangs of any snake on Earth.

HYENA
This scavenger animal is a skilled hunter but often eats scraps left by other hunters of the savanna.

● Animal at risk

ANIMAL BITES

THE ACACIA TREE SURVIVES
DROUGHT BECAUSE ITS
LONG ROOTS
REACH WATER SOURCES
DEEP
UNDERGROUND.

IMPALA
Male impalas use their long horns to fight other males for territory and control of the herd.

WILDEBEEST
Also known as a gnu, this member of the antelope family grazes in large herds on the savanna.

AFRICAN ELEPHANT
The largest land animals on Earth, African elephants use their trunks to spray water to keep cool.

SAVANNA HARE
Keen hearing and smell help the savanna hare avoid predators. Hares eat leaves, roots, berries, and bark.

THE SAHARA DESERT

The Sahara, the largest hot desert on Earth, is covered by sand sheets and dunes, gravel plains, and even mountains. In oasis depressions, water from deep beneath the desert reaches the surface, making life in the desert possible. Here are some of the animals that live in the Sahara.

AFRICA

EQUATOR

ATLANTIC OCEAN

■ Sahara

0   1,000 miles
0   1,000 kilometers

Sand Dunes

Palm Trees

Water

A DESERT OASIS

GOLDEN JACKAL
This jackal is an opportunistic eater—meaning it will eat any food, plant or animal, that is available.

FENNEC FOX
This tiny fox has bat-like ears that radiate heat and help it stay cool in the desert heat.

SAND VIPER
This snake often lies buried in the sand. Although its bite is painful, it is not usually deadly.

● Animal at risk

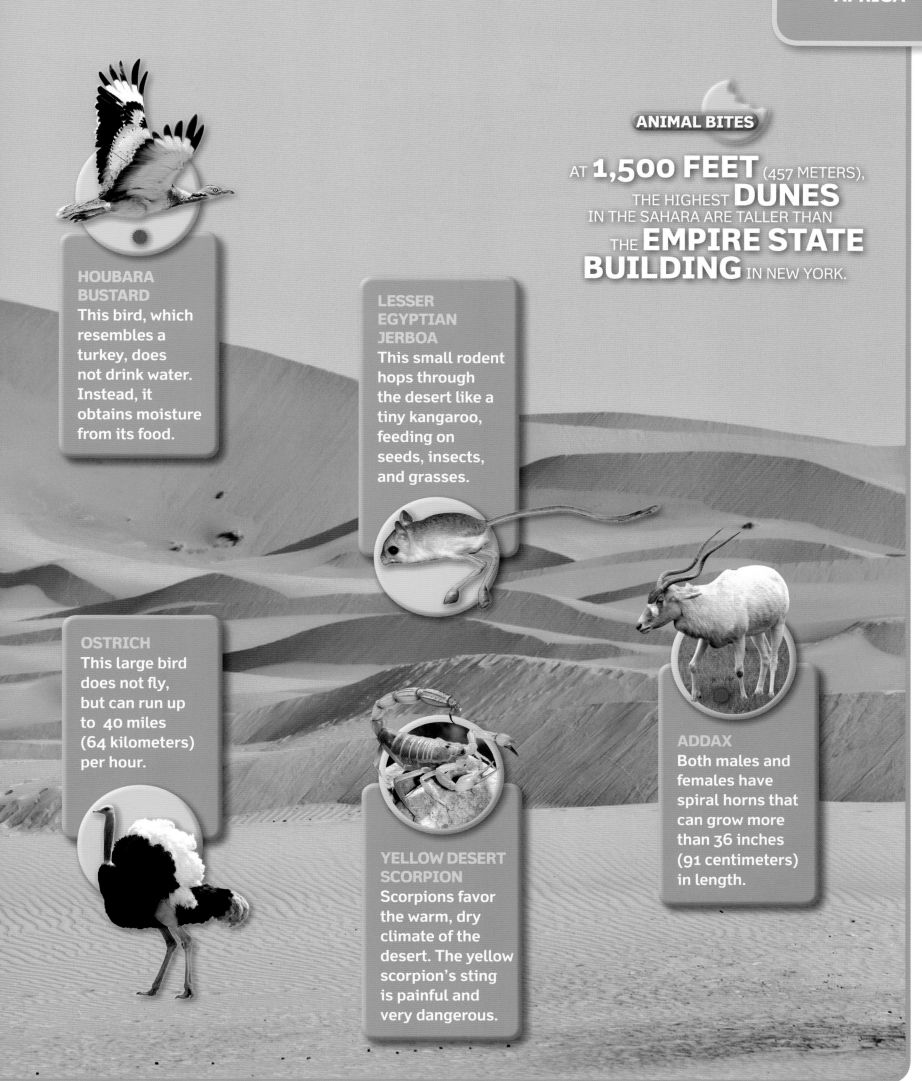

ANIMAL BITES

AT **1,500 FEET** (457 METERS), THE HIGHEST **DUNES** IN THE SAHARA ARE TALLER THAN THE **EMPIRE STATE BUILDING** IN NEW YORK.

HOUBARA BUSTARD
This bird, which resembles a turkey, does not drink water. Instead, it obtains moisture from its food.

LESSER EGYPTIAN JERBOA
This small rodent hops through the desert like a tiny kangaroo, feeding on seeds, insects, and grasses.

OSTRICH
This large bird does not fly, but can run up to 40 miles (64 kilometers) per hour.

YELLOW DESERT SCORPION
Scorpions favor the warm, dry climate of the desert. The yellow scorpion's sting is painful and very dangerous.

ADDAX
Both males and females have spiral horns that can grow more than 36 inches (91 centimeters) in length.

CHEETAHS

The cheetah is built for speed. It is the fastest land mammal on Earth and can rival a sports car by reaching speeds up to 60 miles (96 kilometers) per hour in just seconds. This speed plus the ability to turn quickly makes the cheetah a very effective hunter. The cheetah also has sharp eyesight that enables it to spot prey from a distance. The cheetah's coarse, short hair is tan with round black spots, which helps it blend into the grass as it hunts.

Young cheetahs use their claws and natural agility to climb a tree as they compete for territory in the African savanna.

AFRICA

ATLANTIC OCEAN

Cheetah range

0   1,000 miles

0   1,000 kilometers

HABITAT Cheetahs were once found throughout Africa and Asia, but today they are found mainly in countries of sub-Saharan Africa, with a very small population also remaining in Iran. They live in grassland areas where there is a steady food supply.

DIET The main food of cheetahs is small antelopes, as well as other small game animals and birds that live in the grasslands and savanna areas of sub-Saharan Africa.

SURVIVAL Cheetahs are the most endangered member of the cat family in Africa. They are at risk due to illegal hunting and loss of habitat as farmers and herders expand into the cheetah's natural territory. Approximately 10,000 cheetahs remain in the wild, with the largest population being found in Namibia.

FACTS AT A GLANCE

RANGE Mainly in the grasslands of eastern and southwestern Africa, with a small, scattered population in Iran

LIFE SPAN About 12 years in the wild

SIZE 3.5 to 4.5 feet (1.1 to 1.4 meters)

DIET Antelopes, rabbits, birds, and other small game

A cheetah cub yawns after a nap. Cubs remain with their mother for about a year and a half, learning to track and hunt prey.

Cheetahs have small heads and prominent eyes. Unique teardrop-shaped lines extend from the corner of the eyes to the mouth. This mark distinguishes cheetahs from leopards.

ANIMAL BITES

CHEETAHS RELY ON
TALL GRASSES FOR
CAMOUFLAGE
WHEN THEY
HUNT FOR PREY.
THEY **KILL** THEIR PREY
WITH A **BITE** TO THE NECK.

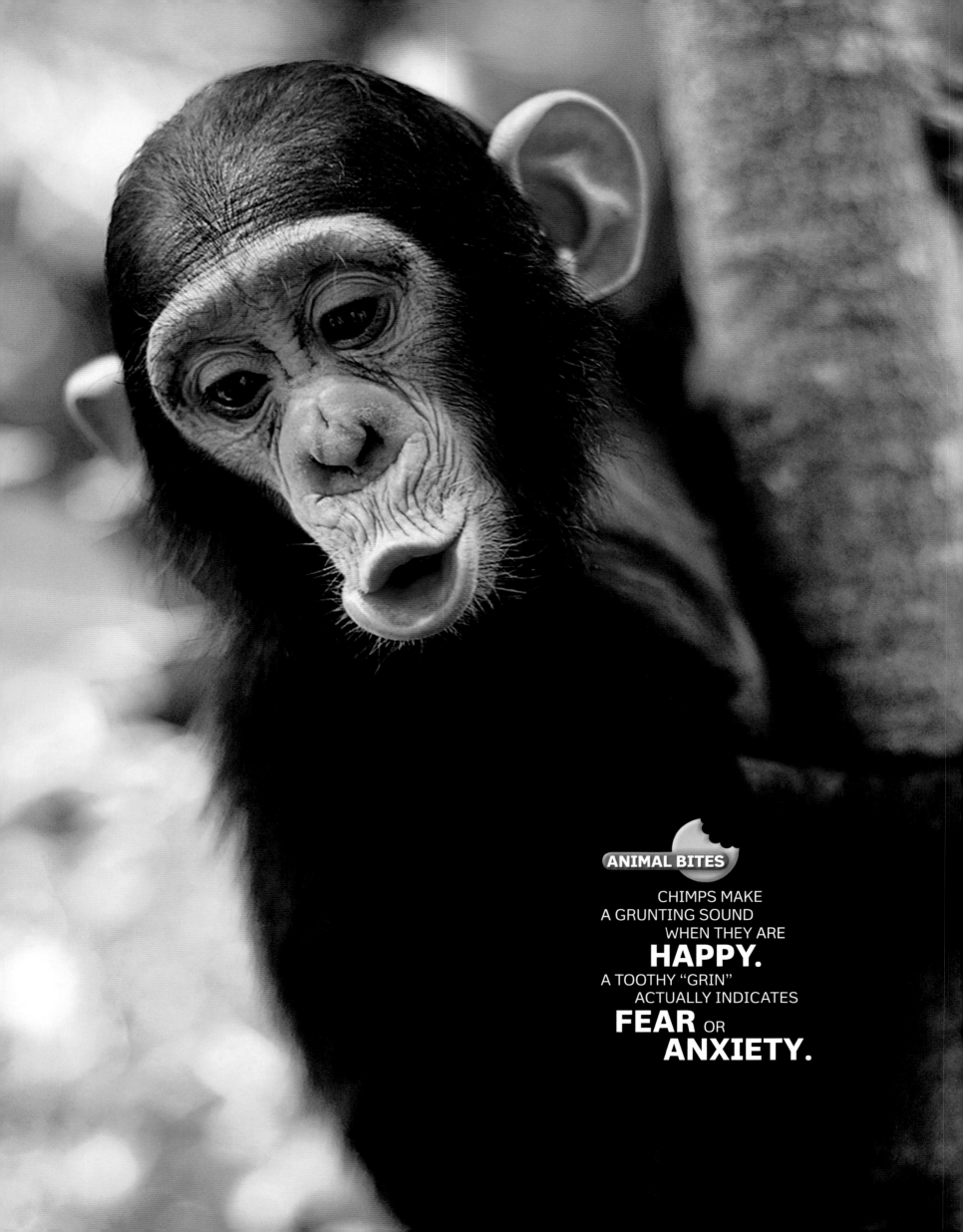

ANIMAL BITES

CHIMPS MAKE
A GRUNTING SOUND
WHEN THEY ARE
HAPPY.
A TOOTHY "GRIN"
ACTUALLY INDICATES
FEAR OR
ANXIETY.

Spotlight on

CHIMPANZEES

Chimpanzees are very intelligent animals. They often behave in ways that remind us of humans. Chimpanzees are one of the few animals that use tools. They often use sticks to dig insects out of the ground. They also use stones to crack open nuts. Some chimpanzees have even learned to communicate with humans using simple sign language. Because they can be taught to perform many different tasks, chimpanzees are often used in scientific studies. In fact, the first "American" in space was actually a chimpanzee named Ham who orbited Earth in 1961.

⬅ A chimpanzee in Africa clings to a tree as it watches something on the ground. A chimp's facial expression often shows human-like emotion.

AFRICA

ATLANTIC OCEAN

■ Chimpanzee range

0 — 1,000 miles
0 — 1,000 kilometers

HABITAT Chimpanzees live in many different forest settings in western and central Africa. They live in steamy tropical rain forests, but they also thrive in lowland and mountain forests. Chimpanzees live in family groups of six to ten individuals. These family groups live in communities that may include as many as 100 members.

⬇ A female chimpanzee cradles her three-month-old baby. Young chimps stay with their mothers until they are seven years old.

DIET Chimpanzees enjoy a varied diet. They mainly eat fruit, seeds, leaves, bark, and insects. But they also eat meat and eggs. Chimpanzees usually search for food alone, but sometimes they hunt in small groups.

SURVIVAL Chimpanzees are considered an endangered species. Expanding human populations have destroyed their natural habitat. People also hunt chimpanzees for food.

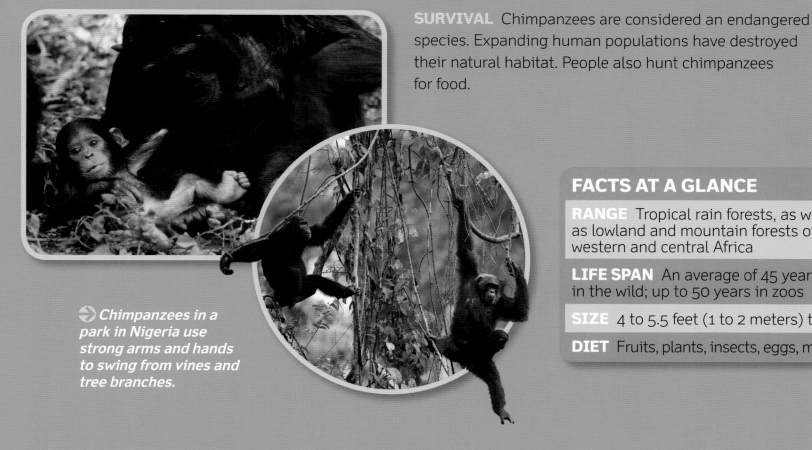

➡ Chimpanzees in a park in Nigeria use strong arms and hands to swing from vines and tree branches.

FACTS AT A GLANCE

RANGE Tropical rain forests, as well as lowland and mountain forests of western and central Africa

LIFE SPAN An average of 45 years in the wild; up to 50 years in zoos

SIZE 4 to 5.5 feet (1 to 2 meters) tall

DIET Fruits, plants, insects, eggs, meat

HIPPOPOTAMUSES

The name hippopotamus comes from the Greek for "river horse" because these massive animals spend up to 16 hours each day in the water. But they are not even related to horses. They are in fact more closely related to pigs. Hippopotamuses typically live in groups of 10 to 30 animals, led by a dominant male. Although hippopotamuses appear peaceful, they are actually one of Africa's most dangerous animals and can be aggressive when they feel threatened.

AFRICA

ATLANTIC OCEAN

Hippopotamus range

| 0 | 1,000 miles |
| 0 | 1,000 kilometers |

HABITAT Hippopotamuses spend most of their time submerged in the shallow water of rivers and lakes, or wallowing in wet mud. Because they do not have sweat glands, they must keep their skin moist to avoid becoming dehydrated.

Rival males, called bulls, open their mouths as far as possible—an act called "gaping"— in a face-off to establish dominance.

DIET The main food of the hippopotamus is grass. They are mainly nocturnal feeders—meaning that they emerge from the water to graze at night. A hippopotamus can eat up to 80 pounds (35 kilograms) of grass in a single evening. In addition to grasses, hippopotamuses also eat fruit as they graze.

SURVIVAL Hippopotamuses were once found throughout Africa, but their numbers are declining. They are hunted for their soft ivory tusks and meat. In addition, as farmers expand their fields, the natural habitat of the hippopotamus is lost.

FACTS AT A GLANCE

RANGE Rivers, lakes, and nearby grasslands of sub-Saharan Africa, but mainly in East Africa

LIFE SPAN About 40 years in the wild

SIZE 5,000 to 8,000 pounds (2,268 to 3,629 kilograms)

DIET Grasses and fruit

With eyes, ears, and nose on top of its head, a hippopotamus can see, hear, and breathe while most of its body is under water.

The hippopotamus is the third largest living land mammal on Earth. Only elephants and white rhinos are larger. Hippopotamuses spend four to five hours grazing on land each night.

ANIMAL BITES

WHEN A FEMALE **HIPPO** IS READY TO GIVE BIRTH, SHE WILL LEAVE THE HERD FOR **ABOUT 2 WEEKS** TO DELIVER AND **BOND** WITH HER CALF.

AUSTRALIA

Australia is 2,970,000 square miles (7,692,000 square kilometers) in area. It is the smallest of all the continents and makes up just over 5 percent of Earth's land area. Australia's closest neighbors are New Zealand and other island countries of the South Pacific Ocean region. Because of its relatively remote location, Australia has many unusual animals, such as these furry Koalas that are found in the wild nowhere else on Earth.

ANIMAL BITES

WHEN A KOALA IS BORN IT IS ABOUT THE SIZE OF A BIG **JELLY BEAN.** IT CAN'T SEE OR HEAR, BUT IT CAN **CLIMB!**

AUSTRALIA

Australia's interior is desert and dry grasslands. Coastal areas receive ample rainfall and have more vegetation. The continent has many unique mammals, birds, and fish that live in different environments.

DESERT Galah Cockatoos live in the desert and semi-arid interior of Australia. This colorful bird generally feeds on the ground, eating seeds of melons and pines that are found near water sources. Dingoes are wild dogs that have lived in Australia for at least 15,000 years. Although they howl, dingoes do not bark like other dogs. They eat small animals, which they hunt mainly at night.

MOUNTAIN Wombats live in burrows in mountainous forested areas of south-eastern Australia. Babies live in a pouch on the mother's belly for five months. Wombats come out at night to feed on grasses, roots, and bark.

FOREST The Brushtail Possum is a nocturnal animal, meaning it sleeps during the day and is active at night. It lives high in the trees on a diet of leaves, fruit, buds, and bark.

GRASSLAND Kangaroos use their powerful hind legs to hop through the grasslands and desert margins of Australia. Male red kangaroos can be more than 5 feet (1.5 meters) tall. A group of kangaroos is called a mob.

WETLAND Platypuses are very unusual animals. They have a bill and webbed feet like a duck and a tail like a beaver. They live in land burrows, but they are good swimmers and hunt food under water.

Dingo

Galah Cockatoo

Wombat

Kangaroo

Brushtail Possum

Platypus

INDIAN OCEAN

Great
Des
W E
P L

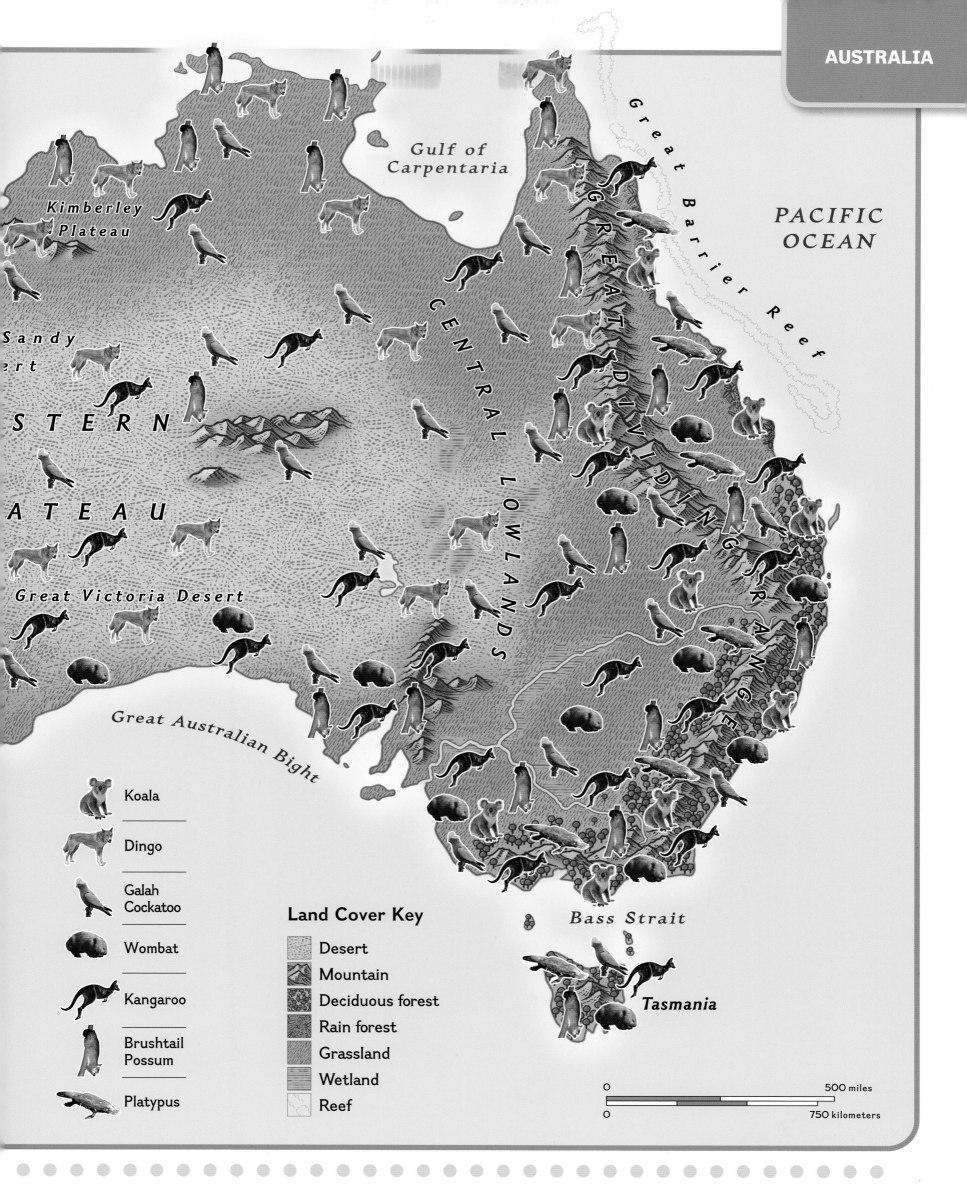

PACIFIC
OCEAN

Great Barrier Reef

Gulf of
Carpentaria

Kimberley
Plateau

G R E A T   D I V I D I N G   R A N G E

Sandy
ert

STERN

ATEAU

CENTRAL LOWLANDS

Great Victoria Desert

Great Australian Bight

Bass Strait

Tasmania

Koala

Dingo

Galah
Cockatoo

Wombat

Kangaroo

Brushtail
Possum

Platypus

Land Cover Key

Desert
Mountain
Deciduous forest
Rain forest
Grassland
Wetland
Reef

0   500 miles
0   750 kilometers

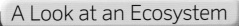

THE GREAT BARRIER REEF

Stretching more than 1,400 miles (2,200 kilometers) along Australia's northeast coast, the Great Barrier Reef is made of skeletons of tiny marine animals called corals. The reef is home to many different sea animals. Here are some of the animals that live in the Great Barrier Reef.

AUSTRALIA

■ **Great Barrier Reef**

0   500 miles
0   500 kilometers

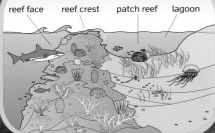

reef face   reef crest   patch reef   lagoon

ZONES OF THE GREAT BARRIER REEF

ANIMAL BITES

CORAL REEFS ARE CONSIDERED THE **RAIN FORESTS** OF THE SEA BECAUSE THEY PROVIDE FOOD AND SHELTER FOR UP TO **25 PERCENT** OF ALL MARINE LIFE.

LEATHERBACK SEA TURTLE
Leatherbacks can dive to depths of 4,200 feet (1,280 meters) and stay down as long as 85 minutes.

BOX JELLYFISH
Stinging cells on each tentacle of this jellyfish deliver one of the most deadly toxins on Earth.

BLACK-TIPPED REEF SHARK
These sharks swim in shallow water, hunting for fish among the coral reefs. They try to avoid swimmers.

● Animal at risk

WHITE-BELLIED SEA EAGLE
These large birds mate for life. They use their sharp talons to snatch fish from the water.

BOTTLENOSE DOLPHIN
These dolphins swim up to 18 miles (29 kilometers) an hour. They must surface often to breathe.

DUGONG
These large aquatic mammals can stay underwater up to 8 minutes while they graze on sea grasses.

ANEMONEFISH
Known as a clownfish because of its colorful markings, this fish lives among the tentacles of the sea anemone.

BROWN STINGRAY
This relative of sharks uses the sharp barb on the end of its tail to defend itself.

THE OUTBACK

The name "Outback" refers to the arid to semi-arid interior of Australia. While the human population is small and mainly confined to cattle stations (ranches), many different and unusual animals have adapted to this difficult and remote environment. Here are some of the animals that live in the Outback.

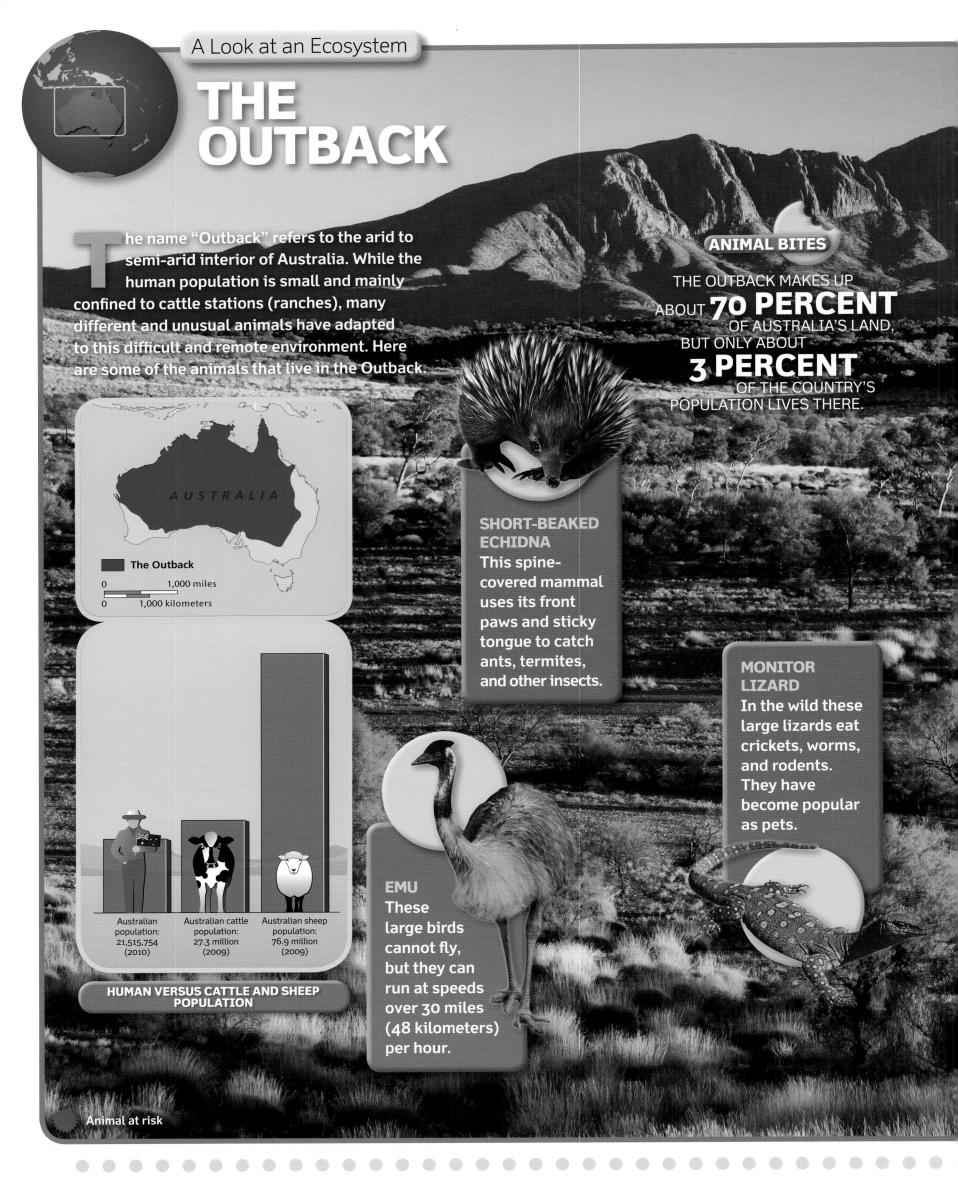

ANIMAL BITES

THE OUTBACK MAKES UP ABOUT **70 PERCENT** OF AUSTRALIA'S LAND, BUT ONLY ABOUT **3 PERCENT** OF THE COUNTRY'S POPULATION LIVES THERE.

AUSTRALIA

■ The Outback

| 0 | 1,000 miles |
| 0 | 1,000 kilometers |

Australian population: 21,515,754 (2010)

Australian cattle population: 27.3 million (2009)

Australian sheep population: 76.9 million (2009)

HUMAN VERSUS CATTLE AND SHEEP POPULATION

Animal at risk

SHORT-BEAKED ECHIDNA
This spine-covered mammal uses its front paws and sticky tongue to catch ants, termites, and other insects.

MONITOR LIZARD
In the wild these large lizards eat crickets, worms, and rodents. They have become popular as pets.

EMU
These large birds cannot fly, but they can run at speeds over 30 miles (48 kilometers) per hour.

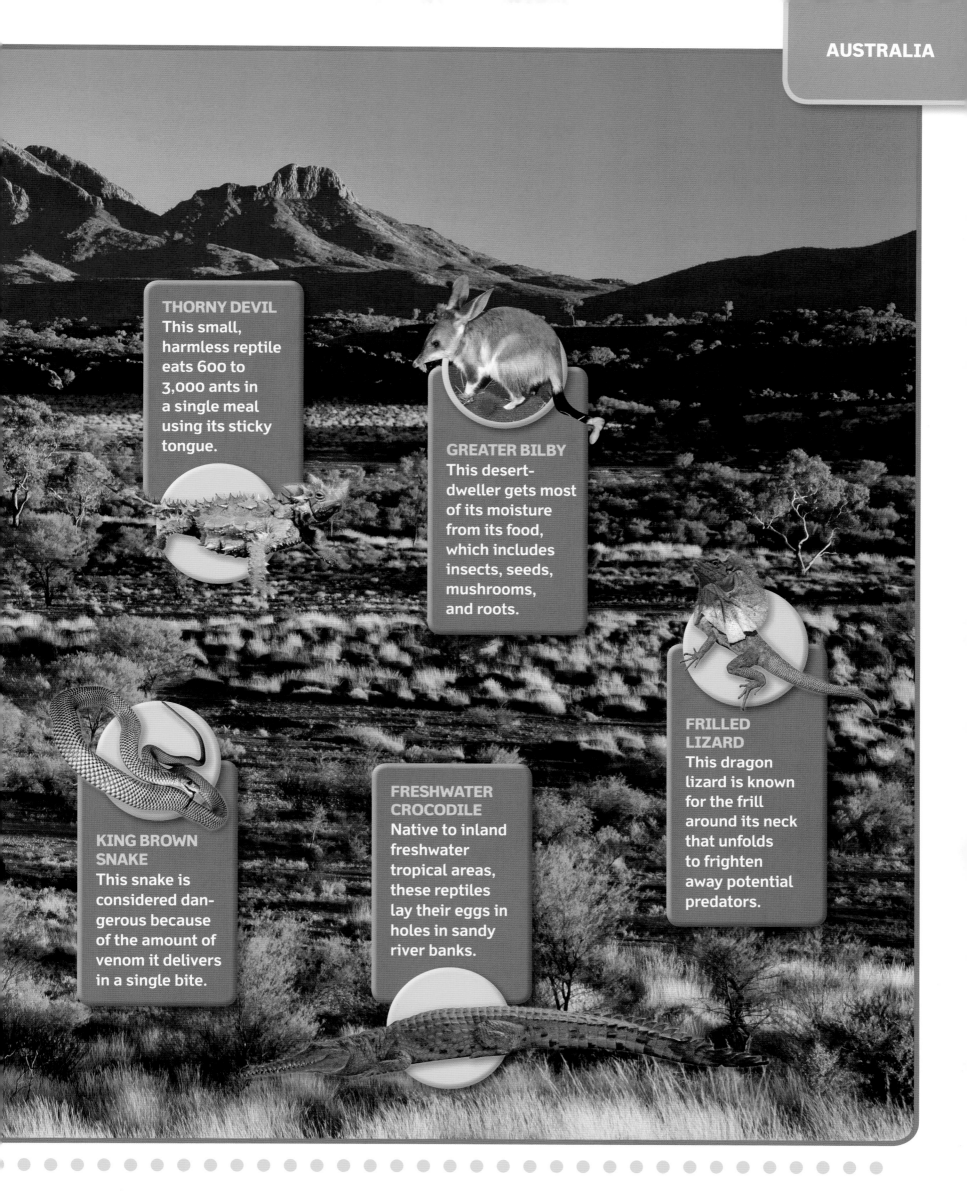

THORNY DEVIL
This small, harmless reptile eats 600 to 3,000 ants in a single meal using its sticky tongue.

GREATER BILBY
This desert-dweller gets most of its moisture from its food, which includes insects, seeds, mushrooms, and roots.

FRILLED LIZARD
This dragon lizard is known for the frill around its neck that unfolds to frighten away potential predators.

KING BROWN SNAKE
This snake is considered dangerous because of the amount of venom it delivers in a single bite.

FRESHWATER CROCODILE
Native to inland freshwater tropical areas, these reptiles lay their eggs in holes in sandy river banks.

ANIMAL BITES

GALAH COCKATOOS HAVE
BUBBLY PERSONALITIES.
SOMETIMES THEY **SCREAM TO COMMUNICATE**
WITH EACH OTHER.

GALAH COCKATOOS

G alah cockatoos are common throughout much of Australia. In the wild they live in large flocks, putting on spectacular aerial shows in the evening as they fly through the trees and dive toward the ground. Like other members of the parrot family, Galah cockatoos are very smart and can be taught to talk. They are friendly, energetic, and even affectionate.

The Galah is also known as the roseate cockatoo. It has bright pink feathers on its breast and the underside of its wings in contrast to its gray back.

Male cockatoos often put on quite a show during mating season. They raise their crest and fluff their feathers to impress the females.

Galah cockatoo range

0 1,000 miles

0 1,000 kilometers

HABITAT Galah cockatoos live throughout Australia, except in the driest areas of the interior or coast. They favor grasslands and open woodlands. They build their nests in hollow trees, especially eucalyptus trees. Flocks of galah cockatoos are also found in parks and gardens in urban areas.

DIET In the wild, Galah cockatoos eat a varied diet of seeds, grain, roots, green shoots, leaf buds, and insects and their larvae. They generally eat in the early morning and late afternoon. In captivity these birds, like humans, benefit from a low-fat diet.

SURVIVAL Galah cockatoos are not considered endangered; however, they are often killed by farmers because flocks of the birds can be very destructive to crops.

FACTS AT A GLANCE

RANGE Widespread in the open countryside throughout Australia

LIFE SPAN 40 to 50 years

SIZE Average 12 to 14 inches (30 to 36 centimeters)

DIET Vegetables, grains, seeds, leaf buds, and insects

A Galah cockatoo picks through a bale of straw looking for grain and other tasty morsels that may be caught in the straw.

KANGAROOS

Kangaroos are the only large animals on Earth that travel by hopping across the landscape. Red kangaroos, the largest of all kangaroos, are known to cover up to 25 feet (almost 8 meters) and jump up to 6 feet (almost 2 meters) high in a single leap. Throughout Australia, there are many different types of kangaroos, including the wallaby, a smaller relative. Kangaroos, along with koalas and wombats, belong to the marsupial family of animals. This means that after the young are born, they live in a pouch on the mother's belly until they are old enough to live on their own. At birth, a baby kangaroo is only about the size of a cherry.

While balancing on their tails, male kangaroos use their short front legs and strong hind legs to "box" with other males.

AUSTRALIA

Kangaroo range

| 0 | 1,000 miles |
| 0 | 1,000 kilometers |

HABITAT Kangaroos live in many different environments throughout Australia. They can be found in forests and grasslands, as well as in the desert of interior Australia and the tropical forests of northern Australia. Kangaroos live in groups, called mobs, of only a few members or as many as 100 animals.

DIET Kangaroos are herbivores, meaning they eat only plant material. Much like cattle and sheep, they graze mainly on grasses but also eat leaves, shrubs, and twigs. They have specially adapted teeth for chewing grasses and stems.

SURVIVAL
Kangaroos are found throughout Australia, but they are increasingly at risk due to loss of habitat as humans develop more and more land. In addition, kangaroo meat is becoming a popular human food.

FACTS AT A GLANCE

RANGE Only in Australia in the wild; adapted to various environments, including forests, grasslands, and deserts

LIFE SPAN Up to 23 years in the wild

SIZE 3 to 5 feet (1 to almost 2 meters) tall

DIET Grasses, leaves, shrubs, twigs

Kangaroos use their powerful hind legs to hop across the landscape at more than 30 miles (48 kilometers) an hour.

A young kangaroo, called a joey, peeks from its mother's pouch. Babies spend up to 9 months in the pouch, living on the mother's milk.

ANIMAL BITES

KANGAROOS HAVE PLENTY OF **NICKNAMES.** A **FEMALE** IS CALLED A DOE, FLYER, JILL, OR ROO. A **MALE** KANGAROO IS CALLED A BUCK, BOOMER, JACK, OR OLD MAN.

ANIMAL BITES

IT TAKES ABOUT
14 DAYS
FOR A **WOMBAT**
TO DIGEST A TYPICAL
MEAL.

Spotlight on

WOMBATS

⬅ *Wombats are generally nocturnal feeders—meaning they eat mainly at night. They typically spend many hours each night browsing for food near their burrows.*

Wombats are the world's largest burrowing animals. They live in tunnels that can reach up to 100 feet (30 meters) in length. Like kangaroos, wombats are marsupials. This means that their young are not fully developed when they are born. The tiny baby—about the size of a jelly bean—crawls into a pouch on the mother's belly and remains there for about eight months until it is large enough to move about on its own.

AUSTRALIA

■ Wombat range

| 0 | 1,000 miles |
| 0 | 1,000 kilometers |

HABITAT Wombats are found throughout southeastern Australia in the states of New South Wales, Victoria, and Tasmania. They prefer grasslands or wooded areas where the soil allows them to dig burrows. They especially like to dig burrows in the moist soil under trees near creek beds.

⬅ *Wombats are short but very muscular animals. They range in color from gray or black to shades of tan or brown.*

DIET Wombats are herbivorous—meaning that they eat only grass and other plant material such as shrubs, roots, bark, and moss. Wombats have long, sharp claws that they use to dig up plants. They also have long, continuously growing front teeth that they use for gnawing.

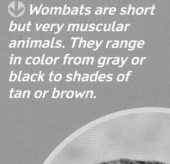

SURVIVAL Some species of wombats are critically endangered. Other species are quite widespread and even considered to be pests. However, all wombats face problems as people increasingly expand into their natural habitat.

FACTS AT A GLANCE

RANGE Grasslands and eucalyptus forests of southeastern Australia, including Tasmania

LIFE SPAN From 5 up to 30 years in the wild

SIZE 28 to 47 inches (71 to 119 cm)

DIET Grasses, roots, and bark

⬅ *A young wombat eats solid food by the age of one year, but usually stays with its mother until it is two years old.*

ANTARCTICA

Antarctica is 5,100,000 square miles (13,209,000 square kilometers) in area. It ranks fifth among the continents and makes up almost nine percent of Earth's land area. About 98 percent of Antarctica is buried beneath vast ice sheets that are nearly three miles (five kilometers) thick in places. Despite forbidding cold and almost total darkness for part of the year, Antarctica has many animals, including these **Adelie Penguins** that live on the coastal ice and water.

ANIMAL BITES

ADELIE PENGUINS
CAN'T FLY,
BUT THEY SURE CAN SWIM.
THESE PENGUINS SOMETIMES
DIVE AS DEEP AS
575 FEET (175 METERS)
AND TRAVEL **185** MILES
(300 KILOMETERS) ROUND-TRIP
TO **FIND FOOD.**

ANTARCTICA

Snow Petrel

Although most of Antarctica lies under thick ice sheets and about half of the year is spent in darkness, the coastal ice and waters surrounding the continent are home to a wide variety of animal life.

KRILL Although they average only 2 inches (5 centimeters) long, these tiny sea creatures are a very important part of the global food chain, providing food for fish, birds, and whales.

LEOPARD SEAL These seals are named for their spots, which resemble those of a leopard. They are fierce predators that use their powerful jaws to capture smaller seals, fish, and squid.

WHALES These ocean giants are Earth's largest animals. They live on a diet of krill, consuming up to four tons daily. Blue Whales are the largest of all whales and live 80 to 90 years. Humpback Whales are known for their songs, which can be heard for great distances through the world's oceans.

SOUTH POLAR SKUA This bird, known for its powerful flight, is a fierce defender of its nesting territory. It feeds mainly on krill, small fish, and penguin eggs and chicks.

SNOW PETREL These birds are named for their snow-white feathers. They feed by skimming the surface of the cold ocean waters.

Blue Whale

South Polar Skua

Leopard Seal

Humpback Whale

Krill

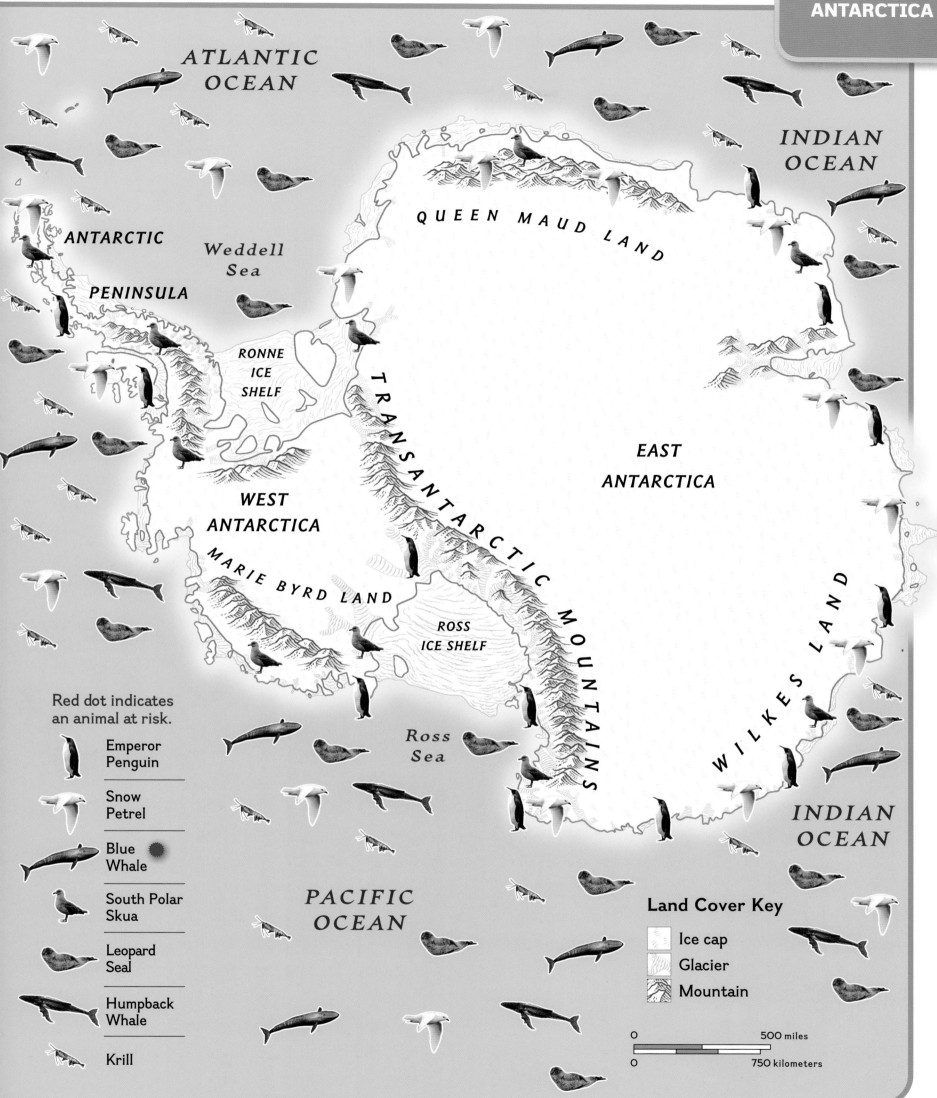

ATLANTIC OCEAN

INDIAN OCEAN

ANTARCTIC

PENINSULA

Weddell Sea

QUEEN MAUD LAND

RONNE ICE SHELF

TRANSANTARCTIC MOUNTAINS

EAST ANTARCTICA

WEST ANTARCTICA

MARIE BYRD LAND

ROSS ICE SHELF

WILKES LAND

Ross Sea

INDIAN OCEAN

PACIFIC OCEAN

Red dot indicates an animal at risk.

Emperor Penguin

Snow Petrel

Blue Whale

South Polar Skua

Leopard Seal

Humpback Whale

Krill

Land Cover Key

Ice cap

Glacier

Mountain

0   500 miles

0   750 kilometers

LEOPARD SEALS

Leopard seals are the most ferocious seals in the Antarctic region. They are the only seal species known to attack other seals. They rarely attack humans; however, scientists working in Antarctica know to avoid these dangerous animals. Leopard seals, like other seals, are protected from the icy cold temperatures of the water around Antarctica by a thick layer of fat, called blubber. Baby seals, called pups, are born with a thick, soft coat that protects them in this harsh environment.

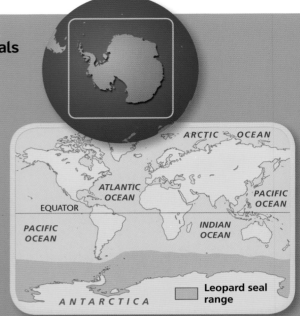

Leopard seal range

HABITAT Leopard seals live on the pack ice around Antarctica in the summer, but migrate north to sub-Antarctic islands during the cold, dark winter. They have even been sighted as far north as Australia and South Africa.

DIET The main food source for leopard seals is penguins. The seals often lie in wait on an ice ledge or rocky outcrop and snatch unsuspecting penguins as they dive into the water. Leopard seals also eat fish, krill, and squid, and sometimes other seals.

Leopard seals have a gray coat with a white throat that is covered with dark spots similar to the spots of a leopard.

SURVIVAL Leopard seals, as well as all other seals living in or around Antarctica, are protected from commercial hunting. The killing of seals is strictly controlled by the Antarctic Treaty. The leopard seal population is estimated to be 220,000 to 440,000.

FACTS AT A GLANCE

RANGE Pack ice and frigid waters surrounding Antarctica and some sub-Antarctic islands

LIFE SPAN 15 to 25 years in the wild

SIZE Up to 840 pounds (380 kg)

DIET Penguins, fish, shellfish, and other seals

Leopard seals use their strong jaws and long, sharp teeth to capture prey such as penguins, smaller seals, fish, and squid.

A muscular body and powerful flippers allow the leopard seal to move quickly under water. It has been known to remain under water up to 15 minutes before surfacing for air.

ANIMAL BITES

LEOPARD SEALS
CAN **CONSUME**
A **PENGUIN** IN AS
LITTLE AS
4 TO **7 MINUTES.**

ANIMAL BITES

WHEN A BLUE WHALE
EXHALES THROUGH
ITS BLOWHOLE, THE
WATER SPRAY
CAN REACH **30** FEET (9 METERS)
INTO THE AIR.

Spotlight on

BLUE WHALES

A blue whale, seen from above, can remain under water for up to 20 minutes.

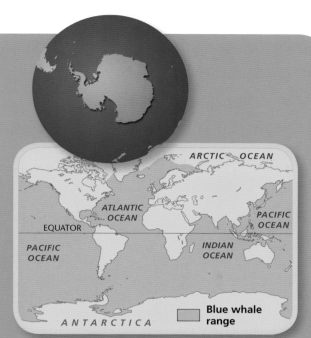

The blue whale is the largest animal that has ever lived on Earth. These giants of the deep live in every ocean, moving through the water at more than five miles (eight kilometers) an hour. Their seasonal migrations can take them thousands of miles.

HABITAT Blue whales are found in all of Earth's oceans, including the waters around Antarctica, sometimes referred to as the Southern Ocean. They spend summers feeding in cold waters at high latitudes and migrate in winter toward low latitudes, where they breed.

Huge triangular tail fins, called flukes, rise in the air as this blue whale dives.

DIET Blue whales live almost entirely on tiny creatures called krill. An adult may eat as many as 40 million krill in a single day. Whales catch their food by diving into a school of krill with their mouths wide open. Then they squeeze out the water and swallow the krill, along with any fish or crustaceans that were also caught.

SURVIVAL Blue whales were once threatened by the whaling industry. Since the 1960s, hunting blue whales has been banned, but they are still considered endangered. Changing ocean temperatures associated with global warming may pose a new risk by reducing the supply of krill. Only about 2,200 blue whales remain in the waters around Antarctica.

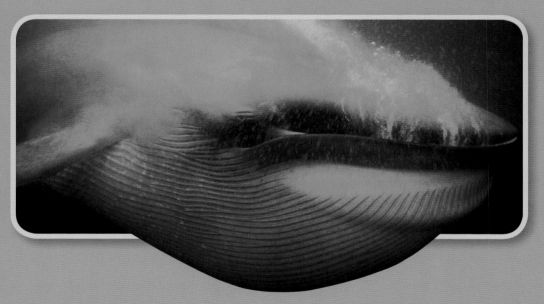

Pleated skin on a blue whale's throat and belly expands to take in huge amounts of water and krill while feeding.

FACTS AT A GLANCE

RANGE Most of Earth's oceans

LIFE SPAN An average of 80 to 90 years in the wild

SIZE 82 to 105 feet (25 to 32 meters) long

DIET Shrimplike creatures called krill

EMPEROR PENGUINS

Emperor penguins are the largest of all penguins. These flightless birds lead a very complex social life in the cold Antarctic environment. Each female lays one egg and then leaves the colony to make her way to the ocean to feed. The males shelter the eggs on top of their feet the entire time the females are gone. The females return soon after the eggs have hatched to care for the chicks while the males return to the ocean to feed.

HABITAT Emperor penguins live on the ice sheets of Antarctica—one of Earth's most hostile environments. During the dark Antarctic winter, temperatures drop to -80°F (-62°C) and winds can exceed 100 miles (160 kilometers) per hour.

DIET Fish make up the main food source for emperor penguins, but they also eat squid and crustaceans. Emperor penguins catch their food by diving into the cold waters around Antarctica. They can dive over 1,000 feet (305 meters) deep and stay under water as long as 20 minutes.

SURVIVAL Emperor penguins mate for life. It is estimated that as many as 200,000 breeding pairs of emperor penguins live on the permanent ice sheets of Antarctica. Because of the harsh environment, many penguin chicks die each year.

ARCTIC OCEAN

ATLANTIC OCEAN

PACIFIC OCEAN

EQUATOR

PACIFIC OCEAN

INDIAN OCEAN

Emperor penguin range

ANTARCTICA

⬇ Emperor penguins are distinguished by bright orange ear patches and a band of pale yellow that extends around the neck and throat.

FACTS AT A GLANCE

RANGE Ice sheets of Antarctica and the frigid waters surrounding the continent

LIFE SPAN 15 to 20 years in the wild

SIZE Up to 45 inches (115 centimeters) tall

DIET Fish, squid, and crustaceans

➡ Emperor penguins live in colonies on the pack ice surrounding Antarctica. They are the only Antarctic bird that breeds in winter.

➡ Emperor penguin chicks are covered with a dense layer of woolly down. As they mature, the chicks grow thick feathers that have a greasy waterproof coating.

ANIMAL BITES

EMPEROR PENGUINS
HUDDLE
TOGETHER
FOR WARMTH, TAKING TURNS
MOVING TO THE
TOASTY
INTERIOR.

A TO Z ANIMAL CHART

NORTH AMERICA: A SAMPLE OF ANIMALS FROM A TO Z

COMMON NAME	HABITAT	LIFE SPAN	SIZE	DIET	SCIENTIFIC NAME
AMERICAN ALLIGATOR	Freshwater swamps, marshes, rivers and lakes	35 to 50 years	330 pounds (150 kilograms)	Meat, sticks, fish, turtles, snakes	*Alligator mississippiensis*
BLACK BEAR	Thick understory vegetation	30 years	86 to 900 pounds (39 to 409 kilograms)	Grasses, insects	*Ursus americanus*
CALIFORNIA CONDOR ✳	Southern central California deserts	Up to 60 years	20 to 25 pounds (9 to 11 kilograms)	Goat, sheep, deer, horse, and coyote carcasses	*Gymnogyps californianus*
DIAMONDBACK RATTLESNAKE	Palmetto flatwoods and dry pinelands of the South	20 years	33 to 72 inches (84 to 183 centimeters) long	Mice, rabbits, birds	*Crotalus adamanteus*
EVERGLADES MINK ✳	Areas close to water	10 years	1 to 3 pounds (0.5 to 1 kilogram)	Crayfish, small frogs, rabbits, mice, muskrats	*Mustela vison evergladensis*
FLORIDA PANTHER ✳	Swamp forests and hammock forests in the southeastern United States	8 to 15 years	66 to 125 pounds (30 to 57 kilograms)	White-tailed deer, rabbits, raccoons, wild hogs, armadillos, birds	*Puma concolor coryi*
GREEN TURTLE ✳	Tropical waters all over the world	10 to 24 years	Up to 452 pounds (205 kilograms)	As babies: plants, jellyfish, crabs, sponges, snails, worms; as adults: plants	*Chelonia mydas*
HUMMINGBIRD	Woods, shrubs, gardens, parks	6 to 12 years	0.6 to 0.8 ounces (17 to 23 grams)	Flies, plants, flowers	*Trochilinae*
IBIS (Bird)	Wetlands, forests, savannas, and coastal areas	Up to 25 years	0.6 to 4 pounds (0.3 to 2 kilograms)	Fish, insects, small reptiles, frogs, crabs, small mammals	*Threskiornithida*
JACKRABBIT	Central and western North America	1 to 5 years	3 to 9 pounds (1.4 to 4 kilograms)	Grasses, cacti, other plants	*Lepus californicus*
KIRTLAND'S WARBLER (Bird)	Pine groves, and areas with ground cover of blueberries, bearberry	5 to 7 years	0.5 ounce (14 grams)	Insects, pine needles, grasses, blueberries	*Dendroica kirtlandii*
LOBSTER	Sandy and muddy areas at the bottom of the ocean	15 to 50 years	1 to 44 pounds (0.5 to 20 kilograms)	Clams, crabs, snails, small fish, algae, eelgrass	*Homarus americanus*
MANATEE ✳	Shallow rivers, canals, saltwater bays, estuaries, coastal areas	50 to 60 years	440 to 3,300 pounds (200 to 1,500 kilograms)	Sea grasses, invertebrates, and some fish	*Trichechus manatus*
NINE-BANDED ARMADILLO	Brush, woods, scrub, grasslands	8 to 12 years	8 to 17 pounds (4 to 8 kilograms)	Insects, grubs, worms, fruit, small reptiles, frogs, bird eggs	*Dasypus novemcinctus*
ORIOLE	Open woods with deciduous trees	12 years	1 to 2 ounces (28 to 42 grams)	Caterpillars, insects, fruits, nectar	*Icterus galbula*
PEREGRINE FALCON	Urban cities, tropics, deserts, tundra	7 to 15 years	2 pounds (0.9 kilograms)	Songbirds and ducks	*Falco peregrinus*
QUAHOG (Clam)	Mud flats, sand flats, Chesapeake Bay	At least 50 years	1 to 3 inches (2.5 to 8 centimeters)	Small plants and plankton	*Mercenaria mercenaria*
ROSEATE SPOONBILL	Marsh-like areas, mangrove swamps, mud flats	Up to 10 years	3 pounds (1.5 kilograms)	Minnows, small crustaceans, bits of plants and insects	*Platalea ajaja*
SONORAN PRONGHORN ✳	Dry plains and desert	7 to 10 years	115 pounds (52 kilograms)	Herbs, cacti, and desert grasses	*Antilocapra Americana sonoriensis*
TURKEY VULTURE	Subtropical forests, shrublands, deserts, foothills, pastures, grasslands, wetlands	Up to 15 years	2 to 4 pounds (1 to 2 kilograms)	Livestock, roadkill, small carcasses, dung	*Cathartes aura*
U	WAITING FOR YOU TO DISCOVER				
VULTURE	Lowlands, open fields, deserts	Up to 25 years	4 to 5 pounds (2 to 3 kilograms)	Roadkill, ducks, newborn calves, small birds, eggs, skunks, fruit, vegetables	*Coragyps atratus*
WHITE-TAILED DEER	Big woods, deep grass, and hammock swamps	2 to 3 years	125 to 300 pounds (57 to 137 kilograms)	Buds, twigs of maple trees, sassafras, yucca, shrubs	*Odocoileus virginianus*
X	WAITING FOR YOU TO DISCOVER				
YELLOW JACKET	All over eastern North America	4 months	0.4 to 0.8 inch (1 to 2 centimeters) long	Nectar and fruit juices	*Vespula maculifrons*
ZEBRA MUSSEL	Still or slow-moving freshwater	3 to 9 years	0.8 inch (2 centimeters) high	Bacteria, blue-green algae, small green algae, and protozoans	*Dreissena polymorpha*

SOUTH AMERICA: A SAMPLE OF ANIMALS FROM A TO Z

COMMON NAME	HABITAT	LIFE SPAN	SIZE	DIET	SCIENTIFIC NAME
ANTEATER	Swamps, forests, grasslands	Up to 25 years	40 to 85 pounds (10 to 39 kilograms)	Ants, termites, soft-bodied grubs	*Myrmecophaga tridactyla*
BLUE-AND-YELLOW MACAW	Eastern Panama	Up to 50 years	2 to 3 pounds (1 to 1.5 kilograms)	Seeds, nuts, fruits	*Ara ararauna*
CAIMAN	Freshwater, rivers, other wetlands	30 to 40 years	15.4 to 127.6 pounds (7 to 58 kilograms)	Insects, snails, shrimp, crabs, fish, lizards, snakes, turtles, birds, mammals	*Caiman crocodilus*
DOLPHIN	Tropical, warm waters	Up to 10 years	187 pounds (85 kilograms)	Squid, small fish	*Stenella clymene*
ELECTRIC EEL	Muddy bottoms of rivers or swamps	10 to 22 years	44 pounds (20 kilograms)	Fish	*Electrophorus electricus*

✳ Red dot indicates an animal at risk.

COMMON NAME	HABITAT	LIFE SPAN	SIZE	DIET	SCIENTIFIC NAME
FLAMINGO ✳	Salt lakes	20 to 30 years	3 to 9 pounds (1 to 4 kilograms)	Algae, zooplankton	*Phoenicoparrus andinus*
GRAY FOX	Lowlands and foothills of mountain ranges near coasts, plains, deserts, grasslands, forest edges	Up to 13 years	4 to 9 pounds (2 to 4 kilograms)	Rabbits, birds, fruit, seeds, berries, small mammals, insects, scorpions, lizards, frogs, bird eggs	*Lycalopex griseus*
HOODED WARBLER (Bird)	Gaps in heavily forested areas	8 to 9 years	0.35 to 0.39 ounces (10 to 11 grams)	Small insects, spiders, and other arthropods	*Wilsonia citrina*
IGUANA	High in tree canopy	8 to 20 years	9 to 18 pounds (4 to 8 kilograms)	Green leafy plants, ripe fruits	*Iguana iguana*
JAGUAR	Tropical, moist lowland forests	11 to 12 years	150 to 300 pounds (68 to 136 kilograms)	Peccaries, tapirs, deer	*Panthera onca*
KINKAJOU (Mammal)	Tropical dry forests, secondary forest, Amazonian rain forest, Atlantic coastal forest	29 years	4 to 10 pounds (2 to 5 kilograms)	Insects, fruit, nectar, flowers	*Potos flavus*
LESSER RHEA (Bird)	Open plains of South America, areas of open scrub, areas of steppe	20 years	33 to 55 pounds (15 to 25 kilograms)	Roots, fruits, seeds, leaves	*Rhea pennata*
MARA (Rodent)	Grasslands and brushlands	12 years	18 to 35 pounds (8 to 16 kilograms)	Short grasses and herbs	*Dolichotis patagonum*
NIGHTHAWK	Coastal dunes, beaches, woodland clearings, grasslands, savannas, and open forests	4 to 5 years	2 to 3 ounces (65 to 98 grams)	Insects	*Chordeiles minor*
OPOSSUM	Tropical forests, southern temperate areas	1 to 2 years	8 to 24 ounces (220 to 680 grams)	Insects, earthworms, birds, lizards, eggs, frogs, leaves, seeds, fruit	*Philander opossum*
PICHI (Dwarf Armadillo)	Grasslands and arid regions	9 years	2 to 4 pounds (1 to 2 kilograms)	Insects, worms, carrion, plant and animal matter	*Zaedyus pichiy*
QUETZAL (Bird)	Lush vegetation, moist rain forest, high mountain ranges	Up to 10 years	7 ounces (210 grams)	Fruits, berries, plants, insects	*Pharomachrus mocinno*
RIGHT WHALE	Ocean waters near continents and island masses	90 to 100 years	79,200 to 160,600 pounds (36,000 to 73,000 kilograms)	Small plankton	*Eubalaena australis*
SOUTHERN CARACARA (Bird)	Desert, grasslands, scrub, forest, mountains, wetlands, farmland, suburbs, cities	Up to 22 years	0.5 to 5 pounds (0.2 to 2 kilograms)	Birds, snakes, lizards, frogs, fish, crayfish, insects, fruit, carrion, dung	*Caracara plancus*
TAPIR ✳	Near rivers and in tropical forests	30 years	330 to 550 pounds (150 to 250 kilograms)	Fruits, sprouts, small branches, grasses, plants, tree bark, melon, cocoa, rice, corn	*Tapirus terrestris*
UAKARI ✳ (Monkey)	Tropical forests and along small rivers and lakes	15 to 20 years	4 to 7 pounds (2 to 3 kilograms)	Immature fruits, leaves, nectar, a few insects	*Cacajao calvus*
VAMPIRE BAT	Tropical and subtropical forestlands	9 years	1 to 2 ounces (28 to 57 grams)	Warm-blooded vertebrates (birds)	*Diphylla ecaudata*
WOOLLY GIANT RAT	Savannas and wet grasslands	3 years	11 inches (28 centimeters) long	Roots and grasses	*Kunsia tomentosus*
X-RAY FISH	Amazon River	5 years	1 inch (3 centimeters) long	Shrimp	*Pristella maxillaris*
YELLOW-FOOTED TORTOISE ✳	Rain forests, tropical lowlands, on the grounds of thick forests	50 to 60 years	25 to 35 pounds (1 to 16 kilograms	Fruit, plants, bones, mushrooms, snails, worms	*Geochelone denticulata*
ZETHUS WASP	Burrows in twigs, wood, or in the ground	4 months	0.5 to 0.75 inches (1 to 2 centimeters) long	Fruit, nectar, insects	*Zethus*

EUROPE: A SAMPLE OF ANIMALS FROM A TO Z

COMMON NAME	HABITAT	LIFE SPAN	SIZE	DIET	SCIENTIFIC NAME
ALPINE IBEX	Mountainous regions	10 to 18 years	143 to 220 pounds (65 to 100 kilograms)	Grasses, leaves, shoots, bark	*Capra ibex*
BROWN BEAR	Northern and central Europe	20 to 30 years	176 to 1,320 pounds (80 to 600 kilograms)	Grasses, roots, moss, fruit, nuts, berries, insects, fungi, mice, squirrels, marmots	*Ursus arctos*
CAPERCAILLIE (Bird)	Evergreen forests in Northern Europe	Up to 18 years	15 pounds (7 kilograms)	Buds, leaves, berries, insects, grasses, pine needles	*Tetrao urogallus*
DAUBENTON'S BAT	Rivers, canals, flat countrysides, woodlands, caves, always near water	4 to 5 years	0.25 to 0.50 ounces (7 to 15 grams)	Small flies, midges, mayflies, moths	*Myotis daubentonii*
EAGLE OWL	Woodlands, deserts, mountain ranges, riverbeds, farmlands, grasslands	20 years	3 to 9 pounds (1 to 4 kilograms)	Rats, mice, voles, beetles	*Bubo bubo*
FALLOW DEER	Broadleaf forests, grassy areas	25 years	66 to 176 pounds (30 to 80 kilograms)	Grasses, herbs, shrubs, leaves, buds, shoots, bark	*Dama dama*
GOLDEN EAGLE	Tundra, shrublands, grasslands, evergreen forests, mountains, wetlands	32 years	7 to 14 pounds (3 to 6 kilograms)	Small mammals, birds, reptiles, fish, geese	*Aquila chrysaetos*
HARP SEAL	Coastal ocean waters near pack ice	Up to 35 years	264 to 297 pounds (120 to 135 kilograms)	Fish and marine invertebrates	*Pagophilus groenlandicus*

✳ Red dot indicates an animal at risk.

COMMON NAME	HABITAT	LIFE SPAN	SIZE	DIET	SCIENTIFIC NAME
IBERIAN LYNX ✳	Iberian Peninsula in Spain, mountainous areas, thickets, open pastures	Up to 13 years	20 to 59 pounds (9 to 27 kilograms)	Mainly rabbits	Lynx pardinus
JACKAL	Dry open country, arid short grasslands, steppe landscapes	Up to 19 years	18 to 22 pounds (8 to 10 kilograms)	Gazelles, rodents, hares, ground birds, reptiles, frogs, fish, insects, fruit	Canis aureus moreoticus
KATYDID	Tropical to temperate environments around the world	1 year	2 inches (5 centimeters)	Leaves of willow, rosewood, and citrus trees	Microcentrum rhombifolium
LAPWING (Bird)	Farmlands, wet grasslands, marshes, pasture	Up to 24 years	5 to 11 ounces (140 to 320 grams)	Worms and insects	Vanellus vanellus
MUSK OX	Arctic tundra	10 to 15 years	396 to 880 pounds (180 to 400 kilograms)	Grasses, leafy plants, mosses, shrubs, herbs, willows, roots	Ovibos moschatus
NORWAY LEMMING	Steppe, grasslands, scrub, open forests	Up to 3 years	5 ounces (130 grams)	Berries, leaves, grasses, bark, roots, mosses, pine needles	Lemmus lemmus
OTTER	Rivers, lakes, streams, peat swamp forests, rice fields, ocean shores, caves	Up to 22 years	15 pounds (7 kilograms)	Fish, crustaceans, clams, small mammals, frogs, birds, eggs, insects, worms, plants	Lutra lutra
PINE MARTEN	Forests with closed treetops	Up to 15 years	1 to 4 pounds (0.5 to 2 kilograms)	Small rodents, fruits, berries	Martes martes
QUAIL	Grasslands; dense, tall vegetation	Up to 11 years	2 to 5 ounces (70 to 155 grams)	Weeds, seeds, small insects	Coturnix coturnix
ROCK PTARMIGAN (Bird)	Alpine and Arctic tundra, rocky landscapes	6 years	2 pounds (1 kilogram)	Plants, insects, spiders, snails	Lagopus muta
SWORDFISH	Shallow warm seas	Up to 9 years	508 to 1,433 pounds (230 to 650 kilograms)	Fish, squid	Xiphias gladius
TUNDRA WOLF	Arctic tundra, forests, prairies, dry landscapes	5 to 6 years	50 to 176 pounds (23 to 80 kilograms)	Moose, elk, bison, musk, oxen, reindeer	Canis lupus albus
URAL OWL	Open woodland in moist areas	24 years	1 to 3 pounds (0.5 to 1 kilogram)	Rodents, medium-size to large birds	Strix uralensis
VIVIPAROUS LIZARD	Meadows, swamps, rice fields, brooks, damp forests, dunes	3 years	11 inches (28 centimeters) long (including tail)	Small insects	Zootoca vivipara
WOLVERINE	Forests, tundra, grasslands	5 to 7 years	20 to 66 pounds (9 to 30 kilograms)	Rabbits, squirrels, wild sheep, elk, moose, roe deer	Gulo gulo
X	WAITING FOR YOU TO DISCOVER				
YELLOW-BELLIED TOAD	Foothills, mountains, forests, bushlands, meadows, floodplains, grasslands	Up to 29 years	1 to 2 inches (3 to 5 centimeters) long	Beetles, flies, ants, spiders	Bombina variegata
ZIEGE (Fish)	Freshwater, rivers, sea water	Up to 11 years	4 pounds (2 kilograms)	Zooplankton and small fish	Pelecus cultratus

ASIA: A SAMPLE OF ANIMALS FROM A TO Z

COMMON NAME	HABITAT	LIFE SPAN	SIZE	DIET	SCIENTIFIC NAME
ASIAN BLACK BEAR ✳	Moist forests and steep mountains	25 years	143 to 330 pounds (65 to 150 kilograms)	Fruits, roots, tubers, small insects, any other available food source	Ursus thibetanus
BENGAL TIGER ✳	Forests, woodlands, tall grass, jungles, mangrove swamps	8 to 10 years	200 to 930 pounds (91 to 423 kilograms)	Elk and various deer	Panthera tigris
CHITAL (Deer)	Grasslands and forested areas	20 to 30 years	59 to 99 pounds (27 to 45 kilograms)	Grasses, flowers, fruits	Axis axis
DWARF SPERM WHALE	Coastal waters near the shore	Up to 22 years	300 to 450 pounds (136 to 272 kilograms)	Cephalopods, fish, crustaceans	Kogia sima
ELEPHANT ✳	Scrub forests	70 years	6,600 to 1,1000 pounds (3,000 to 5,000 kilograms)	Grasses, bark, roots, leaves, vines, shrubs	Elephas maximus
FISHING CAT ✳	South Asian wetlands	Up to 12 years	13 to 26 pounds (6 to 12 kilograms)	Fish and shellfish	Prionailurus viverrinus
GANGES RIVER DOLPHIN ✳	Freshwater rivers in southern Asia	18 to 22 years	112 to 196 pounds (51 to 89 kilograms)	Catfish, carp, herring, freshwater sharks, prawn, mollusks	Platanista gangetica
HIMALAYAN TAHR (Goat)	Himalayan mountains, wooded hills, forests	10 to 14 years	79 to 198 pounds (36 to 90 kilograms)	Herbs and other plants	Hemitragus jemlahicus
INDIAN PYTHON	Rain forests, river valleys, woodlands, scrublands, grassy marshes, foothills	Up to 34 years	200 to 300 pounds (91 to 137 kilograms)	Rodents and other mammals, birds, amphibians, reptiles	Python molurus
JAPANESE MACAQUE (Monkey)	Forested mountains and highlands of Japan	Up to 39 years	22 pounds (10 kilograms)	Fruit, seeds, leaves, flowers, insects, tree bark	Macaca fuscata
KOMODO ISLAND MONITOR ✳ (Lizard)	Tropical forests, tall grasses, beaches, ridge tops, dry riverbeds	50 years	363 pounds (165 kilograms)	Carrion, goats, pigs, deer, wild boar, horses, water buffalo	Varanus komodoensis

✳ Red dot indicates an animal at risk.

ASIA (Continued)

COMMON NAME	HABITAT	LIFE SPAN	SIZE	DIET	SCIENTIFIC NAME
LONG NOSED SPINY ECHIDNA ✳	Mountain forests of New Guinea	Up to 41 years	11 to 36 pounds (5 to 16 kilograms)	Earthworms	Zaglossus bruijni
MUGGER CROCODILE ✳	Freshwater lakes, ponds, and marshes; reservoirs, irrigation canals, ponds, saltwater lagoons	20 to 40 years	1,000 pounds (450 kilograms)	Fish, frogs, crustaceans, birds, mammals, monkeys, squirrels	Crocodylus palustris
NILGIRI TAHR ✳ (Goat)	Woodlands, mountain slopes, plateaus	3 to 4 years	110 to 220 pounds (50 to 100 kilograms)	Grasses	Hemitragus hylocrius
OLIVE RIDLEY TURTLE ✳	Oceans, ocean shores	50 to 60 years	100 pounds (45 kilograms)	Jellyfish, snails, shrimp, crabs	Lepidochelys olivacea
PANTROPICAL SPOTTED DOLPHIN	Tropical and subtropical areas of the ocean	Up to 46 years	132 to 363 pounds (60 to 165 kilograms)	Squid, small fish	Stenella attenuata
QUEEN RED BREAM (Fish)	Oceans, reefs	Up to 35 years	44 pounds (20 kilograms)	Crustaceans, worms, starfish, sea urchins, shellfish, fish	Pagrus auratus
RED PANDA ✳	Himalayan mountains and forests	8 to 10 years	8 to 14 pounds (4 to 6 kilograms)	Berries, blossoms, bird eggs, bamboo leaves	Ailurus fulgens
SNOW LEOPARD ✳	Mountain steppes, evergreen forest scrub, meadows	Up to 21 years	55 to 165 pounds (25 to 75 kilograms)	Wild sheep, wild boar, hares, mice, deer, marmots, other small mammals	Uncia uncia
TUFTED PUFFIN	Islands, steep cliffs close to water with grass and soft soil	15 to 20 years	25 to 30 ounces (700 to 840 grams)	Small fish, squid, octopus, crabs, zooplankton, jellyfish	Fratercula cirrhata
UPLAND PIPIT (Bird)	Shores, forests, mountains	4 to 10 years	0.5 to 1 ounce (15 to 30 grams)	Insects, worms, spiders	Anthus sylvanus
VINOUS-THROATED PARROTBILL	Scrub, thickets, forests	4 to 10 years	5 inches (12 centimeters) long	Insects, berries	Paradoxornis webbianus
WILD BOAR	Moist forests, shrublands	10 years	110 to 770 pounds (50 to 350 kilograms)	Fungi, grains, nuts, fruit, eggs, small mammals, insects, worms, carrion, manure	Sus scrofa
XINJIANG GROUND-JAY	Sandy desert, scrub	4 to 10 years	10 to 12 inches (25 to 30 centimeters) long	Insects, seeds, grain	Podoces biddulphi
YAK ✳	Meadows, steppe, tundra, deserts	Up to 25 years	660 to 2,200 pounds (300 to 1,000 kilograms)	Shrubs, forbs, plants	Bos mutus
ZITTING CISTICOLA (Bird)	Tall grasslands near water	4 to 10 years	4 inches (10 centimeters) long	Insects	Cisticola juncidis

AFRICA: A SAMPLE OF ANIMALS FROM A TO Z

COMMON NAME	HABITAT	LIFE SPAN	SIZE	DIET	SCIENTIFIC NAME
ADDAX ✳ (Antelope)	Desert areas of northern Africa	Up to 25 years	132 to 275 pounds (60 to 125 kilograms)	Grasses, leaves, wood, bark, stems, flowers	Addax nasomaculatus
BEAUTIFUL SUNBIRD	Open habitats with some trees and tropical areas	3 to 5 years	0.2 to 2 ounces (5 to 57 grams)	Nectar, insects	Nectarinia pulchella
COMMON PANGOLIN	Forests, brush, savannas	10 to 20 years	15 to 40 pounds (7 to 18 kilograms)	Insects	Manis temminckii
DIKDIK (Antelope)	Dry bushland	3 to 4 years	7 to 13 pounds (3 to 6 kilograms)	Leaves, grasses, herbs, sedges	Madoqua kirkii
ELEPHANT ✳	Deserts, forests, savannas, marshes south of the Sahara desert	70 years	7,920 to 13,200 pounds (3,600 to 4,540 kilograms)	Leaves, roots, bark, grasses, fruit	Loxodonta africana
FENNEC FOX	Sandy regions of the Sahara desert	10 years	2 to 4 pounds (1 to 2 kilograms)	Birds, mammals, reptiles, eggs, carrion, insects, arthropods, leaves, fruit	Vulpes zerda
GIRAFFE	Savannas, grasslands and open woodlands south of the Sahara desert	10 to 15 years	2,596 to 4,246 pounds (1,180 to 1,930 kilograms)	Leaves, wood, bark, stems, seeds, grains, nuts, fruit, flowers	Giraffa camelopardalis
HYENA	Dry and mountainous areas and grasslands	12 to 25 years	55 to 100 pounds (25 to 45 kilograms)	Mammal carcasses, carrion, fruit, insects, small animals	Hyaena hyaena
IMPALA	Woodlands, grasslands	12 to 15 years	99 to 132 pounds (45 to 60 kilograms)	Grasses, leaves, wood, bark, stems	Aepyceros melampus
JACKAL	Deserts, forests, savannas	8 to 9 years	18 to 22 pounds (8 to 10 kilograms)	Fruit, birds, mammals, amphibians, reptiles, fish, eggs, carrion, insects	Canis aureus
KOB (Antelope)	Moist savanna, floodplains	Up to 20 years	198 to 264 pounds (90 to 120 kilograms)	Grasses, reeds	Kobus kob
LION ✳	Plains, savannas	18 years	277 to 600 pounds (126 to 272 kilograms)	Mammals, birds, amphibians, fish, reptiles, eggs, carrion	Panthera leo
MANDRILL ✳ (Monkey)	Tropical rain forests and woodlands	Up to 30 years	25 to 75 pounds (11 to 34 kilograms)	Fruit, seeds, fungi, roots, lizards, worms, insects, snails, frogs	Mandrillus sphinx
NYALA (Antelope)	Dry savanna woodlands	8 years	121 to 277 pounds (55 to 126 kilograms)	Leaves, twigs, flowers, fruit	Tragelaphus angasii

✳ Red dot indicates an animal at risk.

AFRICA (Continued)

COMMON NAME	HABITAT	LIFE SPAN	SIZE	DIET	SCIENTIFIC NAME
OSTRICH	Dry and sandy areas	Up to 40 years	198 to 286 pounds (90 to 130 kilograms)	Leaves, seeds, grains, nuts, fruit, insects	Struthio camelus
PYGMY HIPPOPOTAMUS ✳	Forests, swamps	Up to 45 years	350 to 600 pounds (160 to 272 kilograms)	Herbs, leaves, grass, ferns, fruit	Hexaprotodon liberiensis
QUELEA (Bird)	Forests, savannas, brush	2 to 3 years	0.7 ounces (20 grams)	Grains, insects, leaves	Quelea quelea
RHINOCEROS ✳ (BLACK)	Savannas, shrublands; deserts	30 to 35 years	1,760 to 3,080 pounds (800 to 1,400 kilograms)	Leaves, wood, bark, stems, seeds, grains, nuts	Diceros bicornis
SERVAL	Savannas	20 years	30 to 45 pounds (14 to 20 kilograms)	Birds, snakes, lizards, frogs, insects	Leptailurus serval
TOPI	Savannas	Up to 15 years	198 to 323 pounds (90 to 119 kilograms)	Grasses	Damaliscus lunatus
UMBRETTE (Bird)	Rivers, lakes, forests, savannas	Up to 20 years	1 pound (0.5 kilograms)	Fish, frogs, insects, shrimp, rodents	Scopus umbretta
VIPER	Rain forests, woodlands	Up to 18 years	15 to 22 pounds (7 to 10 kilograms)	Small rodents, birds, frogs, toads	Bitis gabonica
WILDEBEEST	Plains, savannas	20 years	260 to 594 pounds (118 to 194 kilograms)	Grasses, tree leaves	Connochaetes taurinus
XENOPUS FROG	Rivers, lakes, swamps	Up to 15 years	2 to 7 ounces (60 to 200 grams)	Snails, water insects, worms, fish, tadpoles, larvae	Xenopus laevis
YELLOW MONGOOSE	Grasslands, shrublands	12 years	1 to 2 pounds (0.5 to 1 kilogram)	Insects, grass, seeds, fruit, snakes, frogs	Cynictis penicillata
ZEBRA	Savannas	9 years	385 to 847 pounds (175 to 385 kilograms)	Grass, leaves, wood, bark, stems	Equus quagga

AUSTRALIA: A SAMPLE OF ANIMALS FROM A TO Z

COMMON NAME	HABITAT	LIFE SPAN	SIZE	DIET	SCIENTIFIC NAME
ANEMONEFISH	Coral reefs	8 years	3 inches (8 centimeters) long	Zooplankton, algae, crustaceans	Amphiprion ocellaris
BILBY ✳	Woodlands, shrub grasslands	Up to 6 years	4 pounds (2 kilograms)	Insects and larvae, some plant material and small vertebrates	Macrotis lagotis
CROCODILE	Lagoons, rivers, billabongs, swamps	50 years	200 pounds (90 kilograms)	Fish, insects, amphibians, mammals, birds, small vertebrates and invertebrates	Crocodylus johnsoni
DINGO ✳	Plains and mountainous areas	10 years	21 to 43 pounds (10 to 19 kilograms)	Birds, mammals, reptiles, carrion, refuse	Canis lupus dingo
EMU	Eucalyptus forests, woodlands, shrublands, sand plains	10 to 20 years	110 to 121 pounds (50 to 55 kilograms)	Seeds, fruit, flowers, young shoots	Dromaius novaehol-landiae
FIN WHALE ✳	All oceans	Up to 90 years	154,000 pounds (70,000 kilograms)	Krill	Balaenoptera physalus
GALAH COCKATOO	Open country	30 years	10 to 12 ounces (270 to 350 grams)	Vegetables, seeds, grains, leaf buds, insects	Cacatua roseicapilla
HONEYEATER	Open forests, woodlands	10 years	6 to 7 inches (15 to 18 centimeters)	Nectar, seeds, fruits, insects	Lichenostomus chrysops
INANGA ✳ (Fish)	Subtropical freshwater	1 to 2 years	2 inches (6 centimeters)	Marine insects	Galaxias gracilis
JELLYFISH	Estuaries and in waters along the coast	2 to 8 months	4 pounds (2 kilograms)	Plankton, small fish, crustaceans	Chironex fleckeri
KOALA	Eucalyptus forests	13 to 18 years	11 to 26 pounds (5 to 12 kilograms)	Mostly eucalyptus, some non-eucalyptus plant species	Phascolarctos cinereus
LEATHERBACK SEA TURTLE ✳	Tropical, temperate oceans	50 years	550 to 1,980 pounds (250 to 900 kilograms)	Gelatinous invertebrates, small crustaceans, fish	Dermochelys coriacea
MULGARA (Small Marsupial)	Grasslands	6 years	4 ounces (113 grams)	Insects, reptiles, mammals	Dasycercus cristicauda
NUMBAT ✳	Deserts, forests	11 years	1 pound (0.5 kilogram)	Termites	Myrmecobius fasciatus
ORNAMENTAL SNAKE ✳	Woodland and open forests, areas with loose soil	10 to 20 years	20 inches (50 centimeters) long	Frogs	Denisonia maculata
PLATYPUS	Rivers, lagoons, streams	12 years	2 to 6 pounds (1 to 3 kilograms)	Marine invertebrates, crustaceans, eggs, small fish	Ornithorhynchus anatinus
QUOKKA ✳ (Small Wallaby)	Thick vegetation and moist, swampy areas	5 to 8 years	4 to 9 pounds (2 to 4 kilograms)	Grasses, leaves, seeds, roots	Setonix brachyurus
ROCK RAT	Rocky areas of woodlands, grasslands, and open forests	4 years	1 to 2 ounces (28 to 57 grams)	Grasses, seeds, fungi, insects	Zyzomys argurus
STINGRAY	Sandy bottoms of estuaries, reefs, and lagoons	15 to 25 years	440 pounds (200 kilograms)	Fish and crustaceans	Dasyatis thetidis

✳ Red dot indicates an animal at risk.

AUSTRALIA (Continued)

COMMON NAME	HABITAT	LIFE SPAN	SIZE	DIET	SCIENTIFIC NAME
THORNY DEVIL (Lizard)	Sand plains and sand ridge deserts	6 to 20 years	1 to 2 ounces (28 to 57 grams)	Ants	*Moloch horridus*
U	WAITING FOR YOU TO DISCOVER				
VICTORIAN SMELT (Fish)	Slow-moving water	2 to 3 years	3 to 4 inches (8 to 10 centimeters) long	Plankton, small crustaceans, insects	*Retropinna semoni*
WALLABY	Dense forests, woodlands, swampy areas	9 years	22 to 44 pounds (10 to 20 kilograms)	Buds, ferns, leaves, shrubs, grasses	*Wallabia bicolor*
X	WAITING FOR YOU TO DISCOVER				
YABBY FISH ✽	Freshwater	2 to 3 years	3 to 6 inches (8 to 16 centimeters) long	Dead marine plant and animal materials	*Cherax destructor*
ZEBRA SEAHORSE	Sandy bottoms of coral reefs	1 to 5 years	3 inches (8 centimeters) long	Crustaceans, zooplankton	*Hippocampus zebra*

ANTARCTICA: A SAMPLE OF ANIMALS FROM A TO Z

COMMON NAME	HABITAT	LIFE SPAN	SIZE	DIET	SCIENTIFIC NAME
ALBATROSS ✽	All across the Southern Ocean	50 years	14 to 25 pounds (6 to 11 kilograms)	Squid, cephalopods, fish, crustaceans	*Diomedea exulans*
BLUE WHALE ✽	Oceans around the world	80 to 90 years	418,000 pounds (190,000 kilograms)	Krill and zooplankton	*Balaenoptera musculus*
COD	Waters around Antarctica	30 years	300 pounds (136 kilograms)	Fish	*Dissostichus mawsoni*
DIVING PETREL (Bird)	Southern seas and islands around Antarctica	3 to 4 years	3 to 5 ounces (85 to 142 grams)	Fish, krill, small squid	*Pelecanoides urinatrix*
EMPEROR PENGUIN	Cold waters and ice of the Antarctic	20 years	48 to 81 pounds (22 to 37 kilograms)	Fish, mollusks, crustaceans	*Aptenodytes forsteri*
FULMAR (Bird)	Coasts and surrounding islands of Antarctica	40 years	15 to 18 pounds (7 to 8 kilograms)	Krill, fish, squid	*Fulmarus glacialoides*
GENTOO PENGUIN	Islands around Antarctica	15 to 20 years	10 to 20 pounds (4 to 9 kilograms)	Fish, krill	*Pygoscelis papua*
HUMPBACK WHALE	Most ocean waters	30 to 40 years	65,000 pounds (30,000 kilograms)	Fish, zooplankton	*Megaptera novaeangliae*
ICEFISH	Waters around Antarctica	Up to 17 years	24 inches (60 centimeters) long	Fish, krill	*Champsocephalus gunnari*
JELLYFISH	Waters around Antarctica	Unknown	1 inch (2.5 centimeters) long	Shrimp, plankton	*Arctapodema antarctic*
KRILL	Waters around Antarctica	5 to 10 years	2 inches (5 centimeters)	Zooplankton, phytoplankton	*Euphausia superba*
LEOPARD SEAL	Waters and pack ice around Antarctica	26 years	440 to 1,300 pounds (200 to 591 kilograms)	Birds, mammals, fish, mollusks, crustaceans	*Hydrurga leptonyx*
MACARONI PENGUIN ✽	Rocks and cliffs above the ocean	15 to 20 years	7 to 15 pounds (3 to 7 kilograms)	Crustaceans, small fish, mollusks	*Eudyptes chrysolophus*
N	WAITING FOR YOU TO DISCOVER				
ORCA WHALE	Oceans around the world	25 to 90 years	18,000 pounds (8,000 kilograms)	Squid, fish, marine mammals	*Orcinus orca*
PETREL (Bird)	Waters and pack ice around Antarctica	14 to 20 years	7 to 20 ounces (198 to 567 grams)	Fish, krill, cephalopods, mollusks	*Pagodroma nivea*
Q	WAITING FOR YOU TO DISCOVER				
ROCKHOPPER PENGUIN ✽	Waters surrounding Antarctica	10 years	4 to 8 pounds (2 to 3 kilograms)	Small fish, krill, squid	*Eudyptes chrysocome*
SOUTH POLAR SKUA	On the coasts of Antarctica	11 years	2 to 4 pounds (1 to 2 kilograms)	Fish, krill, penguin eggs and young, carrion	*Stercorarius maccormicki*
TERN	Islands around Antarctica	20 years	4 to 7 ounces (114 to 198 grams)	Small fish, crustaceans	*Sterna vittata*
URCHIN	Across ocean floors	Up to 15 years	2 to 3 inches (5 to 7 centimeters) long	Marine moss and sediment	*Abatus ingens*
V	WAITING FOR YOU TO DISCOVER				
WEDDELL SEAL	Flat, icy areas	20 years	880 to 1,320 pounds (400 to 600 kilograms)	Fish, mollusks, squid, crustaceans	*Leptonychotes weddellii*
X	WAITING FOR YOU TO DISCOVER				
Y	WAITING FOR YOU TO DISCOVER				
Z	WAITING FOR YOU TO DISCOVER				

✽ Red dot indicates an animal at risk.

Glossary

Adapted/adaptation: changing to fit an environment

Animal at risk: animals that are in danger of no longer being found in the wild because of loss of habitat or danger from humans

Canopy: the layer of a rain forest under the emergent layer. Trees in this layer of the rain forest grow from 65 to 130 feet (20 to 40 m) tall.

Carnivore: a meat-eating animal

Climate: average weather conditions of a region

Coniferous forest: evergreen, needleleaf trees that bear seeds in cones

Contiguous: touching along an unbroken boundary

Continent: one of the seven large pieces of land on Earth. These include North America, South America, Europe, Asia, Africa, Australia, and Antarctica.

Coral reef: an underwater formation made of skeletons of coral and other natural substances

Deciduous forest: trees, such as oak and maple, that lose their leaves in the cold season

Deforestation: the process of cutting down forests

Delta: a triangle-shaped piece of land made of mud and sand at the mouth of a river

Ecosystem: a system of living things that live together and interact with their environment

Emergent layer: the tallest layer of a rain forest that grows above the canopy. Trees in this layer of the rain forest grow up to 270 feet (82 m) tall.

Environment: the air, water, plants, and animals that make up the natural life in an area

Estuary: the mouth of a river where the salt water of the tide meets the fresh water of the river

Evaporation: the process of changing from liquid to vapor

Extinction: the loss of one or more forms of life

Food web: the group of food chains that interact in an ecosystem

Forest floor: the bottom layer of a rain forest where fallen leaves, branches, stems and other natural materials are found

Global warming: warming of the Earth's air and water due in part to air pollution

Grassland: land covered in grasses instead of shrubs and trees

Growing season: the part of the year when it is warm enough for plants to grow

Habitat: a plant or animal's natural home

Herbivore: a plant-eating animal

High latitude: the part of Earth's surface that is closer to the North or South Pole

Ice cap: a thick layer of ice on land that flows out from its center

Island: land that is completely surrounded by water

Leeward: the side of a mountain opposite to that against which the wind blows

Low latitude: the part of Earth's surface that is closer to the Equator

Majestic: extremely beautiful

Mammal: a warm-blooded animal that has hair and produces milk to feed its young

Mangrove: trees or shrubs in tropical areas that grow shallow salt water

Monsoon: winds that change direction seasonally, bringing heavy rain in summer

National park: a special area of land set aside for limited use and protected by a national government

Oasis: an area in a desert where there is enough water to support plant growth

Omnivore: an animal that eats both plants and meat

Peninsula: land that sticks out into a body of water and is almost completely surrounded by water

Plateau: a broad, elevated area of flat land

Pollinate: to move pollen from one plant or flower to another

Population: the total number of people living in a country or region

Precipitation: rain or other moisture, such as snow, that falls from the sky onto Earth

Predator: an animal that hunts and kills another animal for food

Preserve: an area of protected land where animals can live safely

Prey: an animal that is hunted and killed by another animal for food

Pride: a group of lions

Rain forest: an area of forest with tall trees near the Equator that receives heavy rainfall

Rain shadow: an area on the leeward side of a mountain that receives low rainfall because the mountain barrier does not allow moisture to reach it

Reptile: a cold-blooded animal that has skin covered with scales or bony plates

Scavenger: an animal that feeds on the remains of dead animals

Shrub layer: layer of the rain forest below the understory with low-growing plants

Species: a group of plants or animals that share common characteristics

Temperate: an area of mild climate that does not have extremely hot or extremely cold weather

Temperature: the degree of hotness or coldness of an environment

Tundra: a region at high latitude or high elevation that has cold temperatures and low vegetation

Understory: trees and shrubs found between a forest canopy and the ground

Vegetation: the plants that live in a particular environment

Vulnerable: animals that are at risk of becoming endangered

Wetland: land that is either covered or soaked by water, such as swamps, for at least part of the year

Woodland: land covered with trees and shrubs

Resources

BOOKS

Earle, Sylvia. *Coral Reefs*. Washington, D.C.: National Geographic Children's Books, 2009.

First Discovery: Endangered Animals. New York: Scholastic, 2007.

Lauber, Patricia. *Who Eats What? Food Chains and Food Webs*. New York: HarperCollins Children's, 1994.

National Geographic Beginner's United States Atlas. Washington, D.C.: National Geographic Children's Books, 2009.

National Geographic Beginner's World Atlas. Washington, D.C.: National Geographic Children's Books, 2005.

National Geographic Kids Almanac 2011. Washington, D.C.: National Geographic Children's Books, 2009.

VanCleave, Janice. *Science Around the World: Activities on Biomes form Pole to Pole*. Hoboken, New Jersey: Wiley, 2004.

WEBSITES

Animal Corner
http://www.animalcorner.co.uk/index.html

Defenders of Wildlife
http://www.kidsplanet.org/

National Geographic
http://animals.nationalgeographic.com/animals/

National Geographic Atlas Web Site
http://www.nationalgeographic.com/kids-world-atlas/

National Geographic Kids
http://kids.nationalgeographic.com/Animals/

The National Zoo
http://nationalzoo.si.edu/Audiences/kids/

San Diego Zoo
http://www.sandiegozoo.org/kids/index.html

World Wildlife Fund
http://www.panda.org/about_our_earth/

Yahoo Kids
http://kids.yahoo.com/animals

Illustration Credits

KEY
COR = Corbis
GET = Getty Images
IS = iStockphoto.com
MIN = Minden Pictures
NGS = NationalGeographicStock.com
NPL = NaturePL.com
SEA = SeaPics.com
SS = Shutterstock

COVER
Sea Turtle, Pete Oxford/MIN; Frog, Tim Flach/Stone/GET; Orangutan, Tim Flach/GET; Elephant, Frans Lanting; Tiger, Tiago Estima/IS; Butterfly, Steve Byland/SS

BACK COVER
Road Runner, Jill Fromer/IS; Marmot, Eric Isselée/SS; Butterfly, Jens Stolt/SS; Gorilla, Eric Gevaert/SS; Ibex, Gertjan Hooijer/IS; Chimpanzee, Eric Isselée/SS; Macaw, Stephen Dalton/MIN; Jaguar, Philip Dowell/Dorling Kindersley; Panda, Eric Isselée/IS

FRONT MATTER
1 (UP CTR), Joel Sartore/NGS; 1 (UP RT), Christopher Meder/SS; 1 (UP RT), FloridaStock/SS; 1 (UP LE), Eric Isselée/SS; 1 (CTR), Eric Gevaert/SS; 1 (LO RT), George F. Mobley/NGS; 1 (LO CTR LE), Konrad Wothe/MIN/NGS; 2–3, Beverly Joubert/NGS; 4 (LE CTR), FloridaStock/SS; 4 (CTR), Joel Sartore/NGS; 4 (RT CTR), George F. Mobley/NGS; 5 (CTR LE), Eric Isselée/SS; 5 (CTR LE), Eric Gevaert/SS; 5 (CTR RT), Christopher Meder-Photography/SS; 5 (CTR RT), Konrad Wothe/MIN/NGS; 6 (A), Joel Sartore/NGS; 6 (B), Ken Canning/IS; 6 (C), Rusty Dodson/SS; 6 (D), Tom Grundy/SS; 6 (E), dragon_fang/SS; 6 (F), Christophe Testi/SS; 6 (G), FloridaStock/SS; 6 (A), Vivid Photo Visual/Alamy; 6 (B), Steve Byland/SS; 6 (C), Sedin/SS; 6 (D), Eric Isselée/IS; 6 (E), Christian Musat/SS; 6 (F), Eric Isselée/SS; 6 (G), Dr. Morley Read/SS; 6 (A), Dietman Nill/Foto Natura/MIN/NGS; 6 (B), George F. Mobley/NGS; 6 (C), Dmitry Deshevykh/IS; 6 (D), blickwinkel/Hecker/Alamy; 6 (E), Derek Middleton/Minden Pictures; 6 (F), Andy Gehrig/IS; 6 (G), blickwinkel/Hartl/Alamy; 7 (A), Eric Isselée/SS; 7 (B), Winfried Wisniewski/COR; 7 (C), Eric Gevaert/SS; 7 (D), Jeff Gynane/SS; 7 (E), fivespots/SS; 7 (F), Sam D. Cruz/SS; 7 (G), Eric Isselée/SS; 7 (A), Eric Isselée/SS; 7 (B), Eric Isselée/IS; 7 (C), Christine Gonsalves/SS; 7 (D), Eric Isselée/IS; 7 (E), Konrad Wothe/MIN; 7 (F), Eric Isselée/SS; 7 (G), Mark Kostich/IS; 7 (A), Eric Isselée/SS; 7 (B), Neale Cousland/SS; 7 (C), Susan Harris/SS; 7 (D), Robyn Butler/SS; 7 (E), Christopher Meder Photography/SS; 7 (F), Sandra Caldwell/SS; 7 (G), Susan Flashman/SS; 7 (A), Leksele/SS; 7 (B), Rich Lindie/SS; 7 (C), Flip Nicklen/MIN; 7 (D), Flip de Nooyer/Foto Natura/MIN/NGS; 7 (E), Paul Nicklen/NGS; 7 (F), idreamphoto/SS; 7 (G), Flip Nicklin/MIN; 9 (A), Hal Beral/COR; 9 (B), W. Perry Conway/COR; 9 (C), Frank Staub/Index Stock/COR; 9 (D), Florian Graner/NPL; 9 (E), Doug Perrine/SEA; 9 (F), Masa Ushioda/SEA; 9 (G), Richard Herrmann/SEA; 9 (A), Flip Nicklen/MIN; 9 (B), Iorga Studio/SS; 9 (C), Ded Pixto/SS; 9 (D), Michael Patrick O'Neill/SEA; 9 (E), Stuart Westmorland/Science Faction/COR; 9 (F), Elena Schweitzer/SS; 9 (G), Reinhard Dirscherl/SEA; 9 (H), Peter Scoones/NPL; 9 (I), Carol Buchanan/IS; 9 (J), Wild Wonders of Europe/Aukan/NPL; 9 (K), Kevin Schafer/COR; 9 (A), Mark Carwardine/NPL; 9 (B), Doug Perrine/NPL; 9 (C), Masa Ushioda/SEA; 9 (D), photo Hirose/e-Photography/SEA; 10 (UP RT), Rich Lindie/SS; 10–11 (CTR), Philippe Clement/NPL; 10–11 (LO RT), Miriam Stein; 11 (UP RT), TTphoto/SS; 11 (UP LE), Michael & Patricia Fogden/MIN; 11 (CTR), SPrada/IS; 11 (LO CTR), Chris Schenk/MIN; 11 (LO RT), Pete Niesen/SS; 12 (LO), Vincent Grafhorst/Foto Natura/MIN; 12 (UP), Theo Allofs/MIN; 12 (CTR), Chris Newbert/MIN; 13 (LO LE), W. Perry Conway/COR; 13 (UP RT), Jurgen and Christine Sohns/FLPA/MIN; 13 (UP LE), Chris Mole/SS; 13 (RT CTR), Johan Swanepoel/SS; 13 (LO RT), NREY/SS; 13 (LE CTR), S & D & K Maslowski/FLPA/MIN; 14 (UP), Tom Vezo/MIN; 14 (CTR), Piotr Naskrecki/MIN; 15 (LO), Delpho/ARCO/NPL; 15 (UP LE), Sumio Harada/MIN; 15 (LE CTR), David Fleetham/bluegreenpictures.com/NPL; 15 (LO LE), Gerard Lacz/FLPA/MIN; 15 (UP RT), enote/SS; 15 (RT CTR), Piotr Naskrecki/Minden Picture; 15 (LO RT), Jane Burton/NPL; 17, Neo Edmund/SS; 17, Richard Day/Daybreak Imagery; 17, FLPA/Roger Tidman/MIN; 17, nice_pictures/SS; 17, Eric Isselée/SS; 17, Gerry Ellis/Globio/MIN; 17, Michel Roggo/NPL; 17, Michael Patrick O'Neill/SEA; 17, Flip Nicklin/MIN; 17, Richard Herrmann/SEA; 18 (UP), Lynn M. Stone/NPL; 18 (CTR), Pete Oxford/MIN; 18 (LO), Wild Wonders of Europe/Sá/NPL; 19 (UP LE), Andrew Forsyth/FLPA/MIN; 19 (LO LE), Tui De Roy/MIN; 19 (UP RT), Anup Shah/npl/MIN; 19, Phillip Colla/SeaPics.com; 20 (UP), Mark Conlin/Alamy; 20 (CTR), George Grall/NGS; 20 (LO), Danita Delimont/Alamy; 21 (A), Wild Wonders of Europe/Allofs/NPL; 21 (B), Lynn M. Stone/NPL; 21 (C), Naturepix/Alamy; 21 (D), Chris and Tilde Stuart/MIN; 22 (UP), Connes/SS; 22 (LO), Gimmerton/IS; 23 (A), Cluck Va/SS; 23 (B), Igor Golovniov/SS; 23 (C), Steve Lovegrove/SS; 23 (D), Public Domain

NORTH AMERICA
24–25, Joel Sartore/NGS; 26 (A), Ken Canning/IS; 26 (B), Rusty Dodson/SS; 26 (D), dragon_fang/SS; 26 (E), Christophe Testi/SS; 26 (F), FloridaStock/SS; 26 (C), Tom Grundy/SS; 26, ND Johnston/SS; 27, Ken Canning/IS; 27, dragon_fang/SS; 27, Tom Grundy/SS; 27, Dave Rodriguez/IS; 27, Christophe Testi/SS; 27, FloridaStock/SS; 28–29 (Backilogramsround), Mike Theiss/NGS; 28 (LO LE), Audrey Snider-Bell/SS; 28 (UP RT), Anton Foltin/SS; 28 (LO RT), Joel Sartore/NGS; 29 (UP LE), Sara Robinson/SS; 29 (LO LE), Jill Fromer/IS; 29 (UP RT), Tony Campbell/SS; 29 (LO CTR), Ronald Berg/IS; 29 (LO RT), Eric Isselée/SS; 30–31 (Backilogramsround), John A. Anderson/SS; 30 (LO LE), Karl Keller/SS; 30 (LO RT), David Kjaer/NPL; 30 (RT CTR), Michael Durham/MIN; 31 (UP RT), altrendo nature/GET; 31 (UP LE), pix2go/SS; 31 (LO LE), Joel Sartore/NGS; 31 (UP CTR), Florida Stock/SS; 31 (LO CTR), Eric Isselée/SS; 32 (LE CTR), Erlend Kvalsvik/IS; 32 (LO LE), Jenny E. Ross Photography; 33, Matthias Breiter/MIN; 34, Tom Walker/GET; 35 (LO CTR LE), William Albert Allard/NGS; 35 (LO LE), Juniors Bildarchiv/Alamy; 36 (LE CTR), Tom Walker/GET; 36 (LO LE), Stefan Gerzoskovitz/IS; 37, Bill Smith/SS

SOUTH AMERICA
38–39, Pete Oxford/NPL; 40 (A), Steve Byland/SS; 40 (B), Sedin/SS; 40 (C), Eric Isselée/IS; 40 (D), Christian Musat/SS; 40 (E), Eric Isselée/SS; 40 (F), Dr. Morley Read/SS; 41, Vivid Photo Visual/Alamy; 41, Steve Byland/SS; 41, Sedin/SS; 41, Eric Isselée/IS; 41, Christian Musat/SS; 41, Eric Isselée/SS; 41, Dr. Morley Read/SS; 42–43 (Backilogramsround), guentermanaus/SS; 42 (LO LE), Philip Dowell/Dorling Kindersley; 42 (UP RT), Dorling Kindersley/GET; 42 (LO RT), Thomas Marent/MIN; 43 (LE CTR), Ingo Arndt/MIN/NGS; 43 (UP CTR), Stephen Dalton/MIN; 43 (CTR), Eric Isselée/SS; 43 (LO LE), Vladimir Wrangel/SS; 43 (LO RT), Eric Isselée/IS; 44–45 (Backilogramsround), Graham Klotz/IS; 44 (LO RT), Gabriel Rojo/NPL; 44 (UP RT), Mike Lane/MIN; 44 (LO RT), Eduardo Rivero/SS; 45 (UP RT), Malcolm Schuyl/MIN; 45 (LO LE), Milan Korˇínek; 45 (UP LE), Francois Gohier/Ardea; 45 (LO RT), Stephen Meese/SS; 45, Jurgen Christine Sohns/MIN; 46 (LO LE), Gabriela F. Ruellan; 47 (LO), Gabriela F. Ruellan; 47 (UP), Gabriela F. Ruellan; 48 (LE CTR), Mark Moffett/MIN/NGS; 48 (LO CTR LE), Joel Sartore/NGS; 49, Mark Moffett/MIN; 50, Lori Epstein; 51 (LO), Lori Epstein; 51 (UP), Lori Epstein

EUROPE
52–53, Dietman Nill/Foto Natura/MIN/NGS; 54 (A), George F. Mobley/NGS; 54 (B), Dmitry Deshevykh/IS; 54 (C), blickwinkel/Hecker/Alamy; 54 (D), Jose Durao/NGS; 54 (E), Andy Gehrig/IS; 54 (F), blickwinkel/Hartl/Alamy; 54, Dietmar Nill/Foto Natura/MIN; 54, George F. Mobley/NGS; 54, Dmitry Deshevykh/IS; 54, blickwinkel/Hecker/Alamy; 54, Derek Middleton/Minden Pictures; 54, Andy Gehrig/IS; 54, blickwinkel/Hartl/Alamy; 56–57 (Backilogramsround), Roca/SS; 56 (LO LE), Jens Stolt/SS; 56 (UP RT), Reinhard Hölzl/Alamy; 56 (LO RT), Eric Isselée/SS; 57 (RT CTR), Gertjan Hooijer/IS; 57 (UP CTR), withGod/SS; 57 (LO LE), Ziga Camernik/SS; 57 (CTR), Bob Balestri/IS; 57 (LO RT), WILDLIFE GmbH/Alamy; 58–59, Paul Oomen/GET; 58 (LO RT), Anna Jurkovska/SS; 58 (LO LE), Igor Shpilenok/NPL; 58 (UP), Juan Carlos Munoz/NPL; 59 (LO LE), John Fugett/IS; 59 (UP LE), David Kjaer/NPL; 59 (UP RT), Markus Varesvuo/NPL; 59 (LO CTR), Bengt Lundberg/npl/MIN; 59, lolloj/SS; 60 (LO LE), Dmitry Deshevykh/IS; 60 (LE CTR), Steven Kazlowski/MIN; 61, Dmitry Deshevykh/IS; 62, Wil Meinderts/Foto Natura/MIN; 63 (LO CTR LE), Torsten Lorenz/SS; 63 (LO LE), Nicole Duplaix/NGS; 64 (LE CTR), Andy Sands/NPL; 64 (LO LE), Jose B. Ruiz/NPL; 65, Dietmar Nill/NPL

ASIA
66–67, Tom Brakefield/GET; 68 (B), ChristineGonsalves/SS; 68 (C), Eric Isselée/IS; 68 (D), Konrad Wothe/MIN; 68 (E), Eric Isselée/SS; 68 (F), Mark Kostich/IS; 68 (A), Eric Isselée/IS; 69, Eric Isselée/SS; 69, ChristineGonsalves/SS; 69, Konrad Wothe/MIN; 69, Eric Isselée/IS; 69, Eric Isselée/SS; 69, Mark Kostich/IS; 69, Eric Isselée/IS; 70–71 (Backilogramsround), Peter Barker/Panos Pictures; 70 (CTR), Eric Isselée/SS; 70 (UP RT), Jeff Banke/SS; 70 (LO RT), Joe Ferrer/IS; 71 (LE CTR), Tui De Roy/MIN; 71 (UP CTR), TSnowImages/IS; 71 (UP RT), BogdanBoev/SS; 71 (LO CTR), Roland Seitre/SEA; 71 (LO RT), David Hosking/FLPA/MIN; 72 (LO RT), Gerald Cubbit; 72–73 (Backilogramsround), Pichugin Dmitry/SS; 72 (UP RT), Eric Baccega/npl/MIN; 72 (LO LE), Bernard Castelein/NPL; 72 (LE CTR), Marc van Vuren/SS; 73 (UP LE), Divashish Deb; 73 (LO LE), Richard Peterson/SS; 73 (UP RT), Maxim Petrichuk/SS; 73 (LO RT), Konrad Wothe/MIN; 74, Theo Allofs/MIN; 75 (LE CTR), ZSSD/MIN; 75 (LO LE), Theo Allofs/MIN; 76 (LE CTR), Lisa & Mike Husar; 76 (LO LE), Lisa & Mike Husar; 77, Lisa & Mike Husar; 78, Bruno Morandi/Hemis/COR; 79 (LO), Art Wolfe/GET; 79 (UP), Gertrud & Helmut Denzau/NPL

AFRICA
80–81, Mary Robbins/NGS; 82 (A), Winfried Wisniewski/COR; 82 (B), Eric Gevaert/SS; 82 (C), Jeff Gynane/SS; 82 (D), fivespots/SS; 82 (E), Sam D. Cruz/SS; 82 (F), Eric Isselée/SS; 83, Eric Isselée/SS; 83, Eric Isselée/SS; 83, Eric Gevaert/SS; 83, Jeff Gynane/SS; 83, Eric Isselée/SS; 83, Eric Isselée/SS; 83, Eric Isselée/SS; 84–85 (Backilogramsround), enote/SS; 84 (LO CTR), Chris Mattison/FLPA/MIN; 84 (LO LE), Nadezhda Bolotina/SS; 84 (LO RT), Eric Isselée/SS; 84 (UP), Johan Swanepoel/SS; 85 (LO LE), Jason Prince/SS; 85 (UP CTR), James Pierce/SS; 85 (LO RT), Eric Isselée/SS; 85 (LO CTR), Mike Wilkes/npl/MIN; 86–87 (Backilogramsround), Seleznev Oleg/SS; 86 (UP), Staffan Widstrand/COR; 86 (LO LE), Kevin Schafer/COR; 86 (LO RT), Andy Sands/MIN; 87 (UP LE), Michel Gunther/BiosPhoto; 87 (LO LE), Four Oaks/SS; 87 (LO CTR), imagebroker/Alamy; 87, Ewan Chesser/SS; 87, Stephen Dalton/Photo Researchers, Inc.; 88 (LE CTR), Adam Bennie/IS; 88 (LO LE), Francois6/SS; 89, Martin Van Lokven/Foto Natura/MIN; 90, Karl Ammann/GET; 91 (LO CTR LE), Jane Goodall/NGS; 91 (LO CTR), Cyril Ruoso/JH Editorial/MIN NGS; 92 (LO CTR LE), Graeme Purdy/IS; 92 (LO LE), Timothy Craig Lubcke/SS; 93, Eric Isselée/IS

AUSTRALIA
94–95 (Backilogramsround), Mitsuaki Iwago/MIN/NGS; 96 (A), Neale Cousland/SS; 96 (B), Susan Harris/SS; 96 (C), Robyn Butler/SS; 96 (D), Christopher Meder Photography/SS; 96 (E), Sandra Caldwell/SS; 96 (F), Susan Flashman/SS; 97, Eric Isselée/SS; 97, Georgina Steytler/IS; 97, Christopher Meder Photography/SS; 97, Sandra Caldwell/SS; 97, Susan Flashman/SS; 97, Neale Cousland/SS; 97, Robyn Butler/SS; 98–99 (Backilogramsround), Dropu/SS; 98 (UP CTR), Brian J. Skerry/NGS; 98 (LO CTR), Ian Scott/IS; 98 (LO CTR RT), David Doubilet/NGS; 99 (UP LE), Four Oaks/SS; 99 (UP CTR), Randy Olson/NGS; 99 (LO LE), Mike Parry/MIN/NGS; 99 (LO CTR), cbpix/IS; 99 (LO RT), Peter Kyne/ARKive; 100–101 (Backilogramsround), Radius Images/COR; 100 (LO LE), EmuImage/SS; 100 (CTR), Steve Morenos/Newspix/GET; 100 (LO RT), Steven David Miller/NPL; 101 (LO LE), Robert Valentic/NPL/MIN; 101 (UP LE), Michael & Patricia Fogden/MIN; 101 (LO CTR), Steven David Miller/NPL; 101 (RT CTR), Steven David Miller/NPL; 101, Dave Watts/NPL/MIN; 102, John Carnemolla/Auscape; 103 (LE CTR), William Osborn/NPL/MIN; 103 (LO LE), Krystyna Szulecka/FLPA/MIN; 104 (LE CTR), Natphotos/GET; 104 (LO LE), Christopher Meder Photography/SS; 105, Deanna Markham/NGS; 106, Jurgen & Christine Sohns/MIN; 107 (LE CTR), Keiichi Hiki/IS; 107 (LO LE), Andrew Forsyth/MIN

ANTARCTICA
108–109 (Backilogramsround), Suzi Eszterhas/MIN; 110 (A), Rich Lindie/SS; 110 (B), Flip Nicklin/MIN; 110 (C), Flip de Nooyer/Foto Natura/MIN/NGS; 110 (D), Paul Nicklen/NGS; 110 (E), idreamphoto/SS; 110 (F), Flip Nicklin/MIN; 111, Leksele/SS; 111, Paul Nicklen/NGS; 111, Flip Nicklin/MIN; 111, Flip de Nooyer/Foto Natura/MIN/NGS; 111, Jan Kratochvila/SS; 111, Rich Lindie/SS; 111, Flip Nicklin/MIN; 112 (LO CTR LE), Ingo Arndt/MIN; 112 (LO LE), Paul Nicklen/NGS; 113, Paul Nicklen/NGS; 114, Phillip Colla/SEA; 115 (LE CTR), Richard Fitzer/SS; 115 (LO CTR LE), Doc White/SEA; 116 (LO CTR LE), AtlasImages/IS; 116 (LO LE), Gentoo Multimedia Ltd./SS; 117, Keith Szafranski/IS

Index

Page numbers in **bold** indicate illustrations.

Published by the National Geographic Society

John M. Fahey, Jr.,
President and Chief Executive Officer

Gilbert M. Grosvenor, *Chairman of the Board*

Tim T. Kelly, *President, Global Media Group*

John Q. Griffin, *Executive Vice President; President, Publishing*

Nina D. Hoffman,
Executive Vice President; President, Book Publishing Group

Melina Gerosa Bellows,
Executive Vice President, Children's Publishing

Prepared by the Book Division

Nancy Laties Feresten,
Vice President, Editor in Chief, Children's Books

Jonathan Halling,
Design Director, Children's Publishing

Jennifer Emmett,
Executive Editor, Children's Books

Carl Mehler, *Director of Maps*

R. Gary Colbert, *Production Director*

Jennifer A. Thornton, *Managing Editor*

Staff for This Book

Priyanka Lamichhane, *Project Editor*

Lori Epstein and Miriam Stein, *Illustrations Editors*

Janice Gilman, *Illustrations Intern*

David M. Seager, *Art Director*

Ruth Thompson, *Designer*

Sven M. Dolling and Michael McNey,
Map Research and Production

Martha B. Sharma, *Writer and Consultant*

Lucy Spelman, *Wildlife Consultant*

Stuart Armstrong, *Map Art and Graphics Illustrator*

Grace Hill, *Associate Managing Editor*

Lewis R. Bassford, *Production Manager*

Kate Olesin, *Editorial Assistant*

Susan Borke, *Legal and Business Affairs*

Manufacturing and Quality Management

Christopher A. Liedel, *Chief Financial Officer*

Phillip L. Schlosser, *Vice President*

Chris Brown, *Technical Director*

Nicole Elliott, *Manager*

Rachel Faulise, *Manager*

Robert Barr, *Manager*

A Note from the Publisher

**National Geographic would like to thank
wildlife veterinarian Dr. Lucy Spelman for her
generous assistance and thoughtful review of this book.**

Founded in 1888, the National Geographic Society is one of the largest nonprofit scientific and educational organizations in the world. It reaches more than 285 million people worldwide each month through its official journal, *National Geographic,* and its four other magazines; the National Geographic Channel; television documentaries; radio programs; films; books; videos and DVDs; maps; and interactive media. National Geographic has funded more than 8,000 scientific research projects and supports an education program combating geographic illiteracy.

For more information, please call 1-800-NGS LINE (647-5463) or write to the following address:

NATIONAL GEOGRAPHIC SOCIETY
1145 17th Street N.W., Washington, D.C. 20036-4688 U.S.A.

Visit us online at www.nationalgeographic.com/books

For information about special discounts for bulk purchases, please contact National Geographic Books Special Sales: ngspecsales@ngs.org

For rights or permissions inquiries, please contact National Geographic Books Subsidiary Rights: ngbookrights@ngs.org